Elvis Presley

© 1990 Benedikt Taschen Verlag Berlin GmbH,
Otto-Suhr-Allee 59, D-1000 Berlin 10

Cover: Peter Feierabend, Berlin
Graphic design: Detlev Schaper, Cologne
English translation: Malcolm Bell, Cologne
Production: Druckerei Uhl, Radolfzell
Cover photo: © The John Kobal Collection, London
Printed in West Germany
ISBN: 3-89450-150-2

The publishers would like to thank the collectors and archives who kindly lent us their Presley
pictures for reproduction. The following photographs were taken by Peter Gruchot, Berlin: p. 121 (top),
122 (centre and bottom), 123 (top), 124/125 (b/w), 138, 140/141 and 142.

LUCAS CARSON

ELVIS PRESLEY

Benedikt Taschen

Ladies and gentlemen. I'd like to do a song now that tells a little story that makes a lot of sense:

A
WOP
BOP
ALOO
BOP
ALOP
BAM
BOOM

Elvis Presley, 1956

Contents

Foreword

"This weird guy walks onstage dressed in red trousers, a green jacket and pink socks; he puts on a sassy smile and just stands there, motionless, behind the mike. For minutes – absolutely still! When he does eventually take up the guitar, he strikes it so hard that two strings break. Two strings! God, I've been playing guitar for ten years now and, in all that time, I've never managed to break two strings!
So there he is, with two guitar strings dangling down his legs. Slowly, he swings his hips, as though he's about to have it off with the guitar. And before the music's even started, the girls are screeching, running to the stage and falling like flies in dead faints."

To country singer Bob Luman, watching one of Elvis's early performances in 1954, it all seemed scandalously improper. Today, 30 years on, it would hardly raise an eyebrow. Red trousers? Pink socks? A suggestive swing of the hips? So what?
Today's pop performers are in a different league altogether. Stage shows are more dazzling and the provocation more direct. Sam Phillips, the man who discovered Elvis, said in 1987: "If Elvis stood on stage with contemporary bands today, he'd look as prim and proper as a virgin." Which makes it all the more difficult – especially for later generations – to appreciate the uproar that Elvis Presley's appearance caused in the arch–conservative years of the mid-fifties.
"Before Elvis there was nothing," John Lennon once said in characteristically laconic and categorical style. But of course

Elvis in 1957, at the peak of his career: two years after his meteoric rise in the charts, the eyes of the movie industry were on him. In Hollywood, he made JAILHOUSE ROCK (1957).

7

that was not true. Before Elvis there were other white country singers who adopted rhythm & blues from the blacks and incorporated it into their own personal brand of rockabilly and rock 'n' roll music. Before (and alongside) Elvis there were movie stars like Marlon Brando and James Dean personifying the wilfulness of a new generation. And before Elvis there was Frank Sinatra, whose appearances back in the forties generated no small measure of hysteria and "the hots".

So we do Elvis and his memory no favours by presenting him as a creative supernova that one day fell from the heavens. Unfriendly critics have never ceased to dismiss Elvis as a second-rate copyist, a good-looking dilettante who happened to be in the right place at the right time and harvested the fruit of other people's labours.

But those critics' harsh judgment could not be more absurd. Of course Elvis had predecessors, of course he drew musical inspiration from contemporary artists – what else would one expect? It certainly does not justify the claim that the fruits of success fell undeservedly into his lap. Elvis's musical talent was and still is beyond dispute; his magic as a performer has yet to be matched and his impact on modern music and society has been immeasurable.

Whether he really made the most of his talent, however, is debatable. Purists claim that the "real Elvis" retired from the stage as early as 1956. That was when he left Memphis and the bosom of the South to try his luck in the dream world of Hollywood, when he switched from the primitive but creative Sun Studios to the faceless New York media giant RCA, when he abandoned the raw, spontaneous, ecstatic music of his early years in favour of a polished, predictable and more commercial style.

One thing is certain: success came so fast and reached such incredible proportions that it virtually ran out of control. No one had the vision needed to steer the Presley myth and no one had the experience needed to bring the legend into line with reality.

Of course, there was Presley's manager, Colonel Tom Parker. He was without doubt a brilliant salesman and worked wonders championing the singer's (and his own) financial interests. But for all his proficiency as a manager and marketing strategist – as a mentor and musical mastermind, he was hopelessly out of his depth.

There was also, of course, the "Memphis Mafia", that confederacy of friends who from the earliest years formed an impenetrable wall around Elvis, sealing him off from the outside world. But instead of playing a cautionary and constructive role in his development as an artist, their friendship rarely extended beyond the receipt of generous gifts. (The depth of that "friendship" was to become apparent to Elvis shortly before his death, when several of his companions sought to line their pockets by revealing intimate details of his life in "sensational" books.)

And there was Elvis himself, the unskilled working-class boy from Tupelo, Mississippi – certainly more intelligent and intuitive than often claimed but ultimately unable to reconcile Elvis the King with Elvis the man. Perhaps anyone would have crumbled under the mental strain; perhaps the Elvis Presley myth was so oppressive that it was too much for any mortal to bear.

Nevertheless, Presley's life – especially in its closing stages – seems to today's observer to have been a string of wasted opportunities and misguided decisions. How would things have been if he had been spared all those (largely) inane film roles? What if he had been provided with better, more suitable song material? What if his agent had been less bent on exploiting his commercial potential and had paid more attention to harnessing his charge's true talents and inclinations? What if real friends had stepped in and nipped his self-inflicted physical and psychological decline in the bud? What if . . .

Those questions, of course, are of purely academic value today. On 16 August 1977, the Elvis saga came to a pathetic end. So let's stick here to the inalterable facts.

His home town of Tupelo, Mississippi, where he had taken part in a talent contest at the age of 11, gave him a triumphant reception in 1956.

11

1

2

3

ELVIS PRESLEY
BARBARA EDEN

Flammender
STERN

Ein Farbfilm der Centfox in
CinemaScope

11

1, 2
Elvis with the people who moulded his life: above, with his parents Vernon and Gladys Presley; on the left, with manager Tom Parker, the man who steered Elvis's career from 1956 to 1977.

3
Poster for the film FLAMING STAR, 1960

Photos on Pages 14/15
Elvis – before and after. While 1956 saw the 21-year-old rock and roll star still bathing in the waves of pop hysteria, his part in the film BLUE HAWAII (1961, with co-star Joan Blackman) placed him in a distant dream world. Between these two photos lay not only Elvis's period of military service but also his manager's decision to transform the "shockin' rocker" into a paragon of virtue.

1, 2
Elvis and women – actually a chapter in itself . . . Above: Elvis in private, with girlfriend Barbara Hearn. Below: His two co-stars in the film KING CREOLE (1958) were – exceptionally – not among his conquests.

3
Elvis in 1965: Records were now mere by-products of a busy movie career. The quality of his Hollywood films, however, sank to rock-bottom. In HARUM SCARUM (1965), he was sent into an Arabian harem.

3

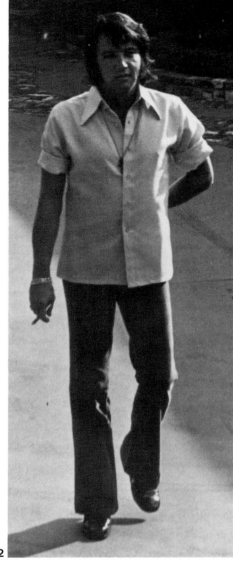

1
Elvis the car freak. He bought more than a hundred Cadillacs in the course of his life, as well as the occasional Mercedes limousine and Italian sports car. His most unusual purchase was a German Isetta, which he incorporated into his fleet in the late fifties.

2
In 1970 in the garden at Graceland. Isolated from the outside world, surrounded by yes-men and parasites, Elvis found himself in a blind alley from which he never escaped.

3
While his mother Gladys was alive, Elvis was a model son. Her death, as he admitted himself, made him even lonelier.

1 1954: Elvis with a home comfort that was most teenagers' dream – a telephone of his own.

2 In the house recently acquired for himself and his parents. The music he played stirred much wilder emotions than the photo below suggests.

1

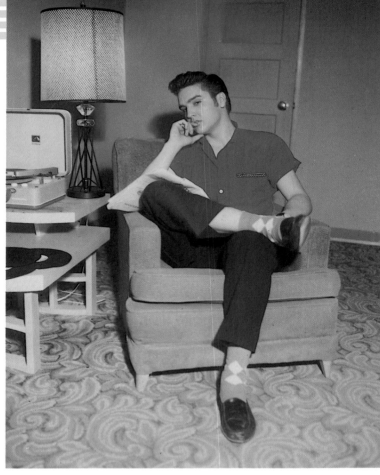

2

1

2

3 A scene from the film GIRLS! GIRLS! GIRLS! (1962)

1 The starting point of an incredible and matchless career.

2 Wearing the typical neckgear of a southern VIP

3 A scene from the film GIRLS! GIRLS! GIRLS! (1962)

4 JAILHOUSE ROCK (1957)

The Early Years

"We had no idea what was going on. I talked about it recently to my father. He shook his head and said, 'What happened, El? All I can remember is me working in a can factory and you driving a truck.' And that's exactly how I feel about it; it just came over us." Elvis, 1956

There wasn't much in the pot of life Vernon Presley offered his family. Often, there wasn't even a daily crust. Vernon had been just seventeen when he married Gladys Smith, a girl four years older than himself. They both came from big families who, for generations, had led a wandering existence in the southern states – constantly in search of work and always precariously perched on the brink of poverty.

Mississippi had felt the full merciless impact of the world economic crisis and the depression that followed in its wake. Work was scarce in a small country town like Tupelo and there were plenty of people willing to work for a pittance as day labourers.

Vernon Presley seemed to be in a rut from which there was no escape. Ahead lay a life of low–paid unskilled work, a frugal existence with few creature comforts and no prospects.

That was the uninviting world into which Elvis Aaron Presley was born on 8 January 1935. The house on Old Saltillo Road had been bought with borrowed money shortly before his birth. Little more than a shanty, it measured ten metres by five and consisted of two rooms with no running water and no toilet. Water was available in abundance, though, when the Mississippi burst its banks and licked around the four concrete blocks which raised and protected the house from the worst effects of flooding. East Tupelo, mostly populated by blacks, was not exactly a desirable residential area. Still, the family had a roof over its head.

Elvis came into the world with a twin brother, Jesse Garon, but the latter died at birth. Later, Elvis remarked: "They say that when one twin dies the survivor acquires all the positive qualities of the deceased. If that's really true, I can count myself lucky."

But luck was a long time coming. In 1938, when Elvis was just three years old, Vernon was sentenced to three years' imprisonment for forging a cheque. Hunger had got the better of honesty. Together with two friends, Vernon had forged a cheque for 200 dollars to pay for a trip to Texas to look for work. Instead, the amateurish act of desperation landed the men in the notorious Parchman Prison Farm, where Vernon served his sentence picking cotton under a blazing sun.

The calamity brought Gladys and Elvis even closer together. While Vernon at least received a hot meal each day, mother and son regularly went to bed hungry. Gladys' relations helped as much as they could and Gladys herself found occasional cleaning jobs and took in washing so that she and her son could at least live "from hand to mouth". The family's plight did not, however, prevent her from showering her only son with love and attention. Elvis was not let out of her sight for a second. In fact, as far as financial circumstances would permit, he was spoilt and mollycoddled, ultimately becoming so fixated on his mother that, when she died in 1958 at the age of just 46, his world collapsed. The maternal bond, however, was cemented by more than just love and affection: Elvis's sense of decency, honesty, courtesy (even at the peak of his career, he would address producers and recording company executives as "Sir") and hard work bore his mother's indelible stamp. With his father's prison sentence fresh in his mind, Elvis entered his teens immune to the temptations of others who supplemented their pocketmoney by petty larceny. A fleeting acquaintance, who himself spent time behind bars for theft, later recalled: "Of course, none of us knew what was to become of Elvis later. But one thing we did know was that he would never join a gang and would never do anything illegal." And there was another factor that played a crucial role in moulding Elvis's personality: the church. Although not overly religious, the Presleys regularly attended services at the "First Assembly of God Church". Every Sunday, the ramshackle wooden church on Adams Street became a place of refuge and moral inspiration – and, equally important for Elvis, a place of musical training.

The white Baptist congregation in the heart of the black neighbourhood was powered by a bizarre mixture of Bible-belt piety and Holy Rolling ecstasy. The church walls vibrated to resounding deliveries of gospel chorals and spirituals and the preacher bore a closer resemblance to a pagan shaman than a church dignitary.

Elvis was fascinated: "Even at two years of age, gospel music played a tremendously important part in my life. My mother told me that I would jump off her lap, run up to the front and start to sing. Even if I didn't understand the words, I at least knew the melody. And even though I didn't always hit the right note, I was louder than the rest. Singing, for me, was the most

1
The memorial plaque greeting Elvis pilgrims and tourists in Tupelo.

2
The (now-renovated) house on Old Saltillo Road in Tupelo. This was where Elvis Aaron Presley was born to near destitute parents on 8 January 1935.

3
The earliest surviving photo: Elvis, just under three years old, with his parents Vernon and Gladys.

2

3

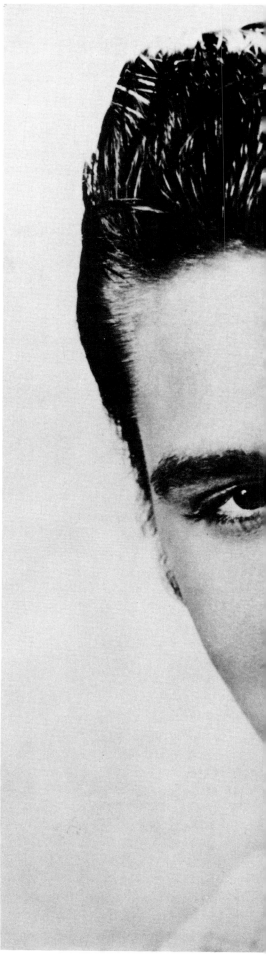

natural thing in the world; it was my way of unburdening my heart. When I was four or five, I looked forward all week to going to church on Sundays with my father and mother."

But gospel music, as Elvis's only source of musical inspiration, soon faced competition. When father Vernon – prematurely released from prison – came home of an evening in the truck, Elvis would climb into the driver's seat and listen to the radio for hours on end. Local radio stations were already thick on the ground in the USA, so the young Presley could certainly not complain of a shortage of musical stimulation.

There were the "white" stations, playing mostly country and western music with artists like Jimmie Rodgers, Bob Wills, Ernest Tubb and Roy Acuff. And there were the "black" stations, which naturally gave most air time to coloured musicians: John Lee Hooker, Howlin' Wolf, Muddy Waters, Bukka

By today's standards, the mid-fifties rebel looks almost respectable. Many portraits conceal the carnal aura which many puritanical Americans found obscene: Elvis as the nice boy next door.

White, Big Bill Broonzy, B.B. King, Otis Span and all the other artists who put the rural "Mississippi Delta Blues" and its urban counterpart, the "Chicago Blues", on the musical map. Elvis, untainted by racial prejudice, eagerly took it all in. And in the process – perhaps it was the thrill of forbidden fruit – he developed a secret preference for the black man's blues and rhythm & blues, music disparagingly labelled "race music" by the whites.

Before young Presley's own meteoric rise in the music world, though, humdrum hurdles such as schooling had to be overcome. In September 1941, Elvis was enrolled at the "East Tupelo Consolidated School". No one recalls his early school days; courteous and quiet as ever, he was neither an academic achiever nor a classroom prankster. "He was a well-behaved little boy," said his teacher, Mrs Grimes, "well-behaved and of average ability."

One talent, though, did not escape Mrs Grimes's educational eye – or rather ear. One day, when she asked the class at morning prayers whether anyone had a prayer to offer, ten-year-old Elvis stood up and started to sing. Mrs Grimes was so overwhelmed that she told the school principal. He – no less impressed – sent Elvis to represent East Tupelo at the "Mississippi-Alabama Fair and Dairy Show", one of the biggest events in the local farming and social calendar. Aside from cattle and horse auctions, its attractions included talent competitions and beauty contests. With a rendering of the touching folk ballad "Old Shep" – which he sang without instrumental accompaniment, as at school – Elvis won second prize in the talent contest: five dollars and a day's free admission to all the fairground attractions.

Perhaps it was that experience as a ten-year-old that sowed the seeds of desire for a career on the stage in later life. There is no corroborative evidence, though, of Elvis harbouring any such early ambition.

Nevertheless, he was not overly disappointed when his 11th birthday present turned out to be not the bicycle he'd asked for but a guitar. His parents, with a joint monthly income of 140 dollars at most, simply couldn't afford the 55 dollars for a bicycle. Even scraping together 12 dollars for a guitar meant making sacrifices elsewhere: Vernon had to give up his beloved cigarettes for several weeks.

Elvis devoted himself to the guitar. He learnt a few chords from members of the family and tried to copy what he heard on the radio. By the age of thirteen, he had made so much progress that the children of the neighbourhood would gather behind the Presleys' house to listen to Elvis singing and playing.

The shy, lacklustre little boy slowly came out of his shell, discovering music as an ideal vehicle for overcoming inhibitions and making friends. But just as he was starting, as it were, to blossom inside, he was once again uprooted: the Presleys moved to Memphis.

2

In the years prior to the move, Vernon Presley had frequently jobbed in Memphis, travelling 170 kilometres back and forth from Tupelo.

In the late war years, Tennessee's biggest city (population at the time: 300,000) offered more work than the sleepy township of Tupelo and Vernon had hopes of finally landing a secure job. "We were broke, flat broke," Elvis recalled later. "We cut and ran overnight. Pa packed the boxes with our belongings onto the '39 Plymouth and hit the road. Things could only get better."

But things only got worse. When the Presleys arrived in Memphis in September '48, they had to make do with a squalid one-room apartment in the slums. The search for work also proved harder than expected. Gladys helped out again by working as a seamstress and shop assistant while Vernon tried to make ends meet as a trucker and casual labourer.

In 1949, he did eventually find a job that he was to keep for the next five years. At the "United Paint Company" he earned an acceptable 40 dollars a week, which soon enabled the Presleys to move to more salubrious accommodation.

1
The Elvis the public never saw: he would often sit down at the piano alone to play gospel songs and spirituals.

2
Elvis in Hollywood. One of the countless MGM publicity photos showing the fledgling filmstar during the making of JAILHOUSE ROCK (1957)

Photo on Page 32/33:
Elvis taking a break from work with Sonny Neal, the son of his first manager Bob Neal, at a lake near Memphis.

31

For Elvis, the dust stirred up by the move took several agonizing months to settle. At Humes High School, he found himself among 1 600 pupils and was horrified by the initial experience – especially since his physical appearance tended to trigger aggression in his peers. Elvis liked to wear garishly coloured clothes and was the only boy in the school who let his hair grow and wore long sideburns like a trucker. "One day," reports Red West, who later became his friend, "the whole pack descended on him, determined to cut off his hair. I helped him out of that particular fix. On another occasion, the sports teacher wanted to send him to the barber's – otherwise he'd be kicked out of the football team. Elvis refused to go. He was different from the rest; he loved getting people's goat." Elvis continued to run the gauntlet unperturbed. His mother had told him over and over again that he was something special. And now, albeit in an unorthodox way, he intended to prove it.

Once again, it was music that broke the ice. At private and school parties, Elvis and his guitar became the focus of attention. "His voice," said Elvis's history teacher Miss Scrivener, "had such a forceful quality that it drew people like a magnet." Elvis's big moment came at the annual school ball, where he was one of thirty candidates chosen to perform before the assembled audience. The candidate who reaped the most applause would be allowed to mount the stage a second time. When Elvis (who else!) left the stage after the encore, even he was speechless. "I'll never forget the expression on his face. 'They like me, Miss Scrivener, they really like me.'"

When he left Humes High in 1953, Elvis was no longer seen as a weird outsider; he had lots of friends and was particularly popular with the opposite sex. "He loved dating girls", said his former school friend Buzzy Forbes, "and he was damned successful. The girls were crazy about him. At parties, he was always the centre of attention."

And it was because of a girl that he lost his first job. While he was still at school, Elvis worked in the evenings at a local cinema, the Loew's State Theater. After a fight with one of the ushers, who objected to one of the female members of staff only having eyes for Elvis, the troublemaker was instantly dismissed. The incident did not, however, leave any lasting scars: his fondness for the female sex remained undiminished – and his weakness for the cinema developed over the years into a veritable passion.

But first, Elvis was introduced to the serious side of life. In November 1953, he got a $1.25-an-hour job as a driver with the "Crown Electric Company". His hairstyle and extravagant manner of dress again made him the object of scorn and ridicule, but the eighteen-year-old bird of paradise ignored his workmates' taunts. His dream was to become a well-paid electrician. "When I was sitting in my truck and saw a gleaming new car drive past, I invariably started to dream. Somehow I knew that something was going to happen in my life. What

MODERN – – STUDIOS – – COMPLETE

MEMPHIS *Recording* **SERVICE**

706 UNION   PH. 37-7197   MEMPHIS, TENN.

"Combining the NEWEST and BEST EQUIPMENT with the LATEST and FINEST SONOCOUSTIC STUDIOS"

DISC – TAPE – WIRE

STANDARD and MICROGROOVE   33 1-3 – 45 – 78 RPM

"A Complete Service to Fill Every Recording Need"

form it would take I didn't know, but I had a feeling that the future had a happy surprise in store for me."

The future made its first appearance in the form of a small, unassuming building on Union Avenue, which he often drove past in his truck. Above the door were the words "Memphis Recording Service" in neon letters. Under the name "Sun Studios", this company was to change the face of popular music.

This is where his career started: the "Memphis Recording Service", later known as "Sun Studios", produced Elvis's first recordings.

The Big Break

The business was owned by Sam Phillips, a former radio station employee, who set up the studio in 1951 and specialized in giving young and unknown coloured artists a chance. "It seemed to me that the blacks were the only ones who had preserved an air of freshness in their music. But here in the southern states there was nowhere for them to record their music. And hardly any of them had the money to go to Chicago."

Phillips first brought unknown musicians like B. B. King and Little Junior Parker into the studio and recorded singles with them which he then sold to better–established companies. His profit margin was so small that he needed a lucrative sideline, which he hoped he had found in the "Memphis Recording Service". Here, for four dollars, anyone could walk in off the street and make a soft disc recording – a musical greeting for friends and relations, for birthdays and weddings. One Saturday afternoon in Summer '53, Elvis Presley entered the studio on Union Avenue.

Legend has it that Elvis wanted to record two songs for his mother's birthday. If that were the case, though, he was doing his shopping very early, because his mother's birthday was several months away. More probably, Elvis was using the birthday as an excuse to attract Sam Phillips' attention. Phillips said: "I bet he drove past a dozen times, desperately thinking how to say his piece without getting it all garbled up." Another legend, however, is based on fact: Sam Phillips had repeatedly told his assistant Marion Keisker: "If I could only

This is how it's done! Sam Phillips, the man who discovered Elvis, showing his young protégé a new chord.

find a white man with a black voice and a black feel for music, I could make a billion dollars!"

Those words were ringing in Marion Keisker's ears when she asked Elvis into the studio to record two songs ("My Happiness" and "That's When Your Heart–Aches Begin"). She was so impressed by Presley's earthy, unpolished voice that she made a simultaneous tape recording, which she later played back to Sam Phillips.

Phillips liked what he heard but not enough to take up Keisker's suggestion that he should ring Elvis at home and find out more about him. It was left to Elvis to take his heart in his hands and present himself a second time, which he duly did on 4 January 1954, calling at the studio to record another two songs.

This time, Phillips himself was present and what he heard made him prick up his ears. "I told him: 'If I find the right songs, would you be interested in giving it a try?' And by God, he was interested."

Again, months went by. Marion Keisker recalls: "Every time a new song arrived on the desk I said to Sam: 'What do you think? Shall we call the boy with the sideburns and give him a chance?' But each time Sam would say: 'I don't know if he's ready yet.' or 'How on Earth do we get in touch with him?.' And by the time I'd found Elvis's telephone number, Sam's mind was on something else. Things went on like that for several months."

In June '54 Keisker's persistence finally paid off. Phillips was looking for a singer for a new song and told his assistant to track down the strange guy with the sideburns. "'Do you fancy trying a Blues number?' Phillips said on the telephone, although he knew full well that I was champing at the bit. I only know that I put down the receiver and ran for my life. I was so fast that he still had the phone in his hand when I arrived at the studio."

But the first attempt ended in a blind alley. For three hours, Phillips tried in vain to get from Elvis the kind of delivery he felt the song needed. At the same time, his instinct told him that, in Elvis, he had a rough diamond in his hand; all he had to do was find the right cut. "I knew he was the singer I'd been looking for. He had enormous potential, an unusual voice and a musical background that embraced everything from Bing Crosby through Arthur "Big Boy" Crudup to Hank Snow. But he was also the shiest and most insecure boy that ever set foot in my studio. He didn't play in a band, he didn't go to clubs, he didn't hang around with other musicians – no, he sat on his bed at home and played to himself.

So I thought the first thing to do was find out which direction his music should take. Crooners like Perry Como and Eddie Fisher were a dime a dozen. Why squeeze into a market that was already over-saturated? A cake can only be cut into so many slices. No, I had other plans for Elvis: from him, I wanted a younger, faster, wilder sound."

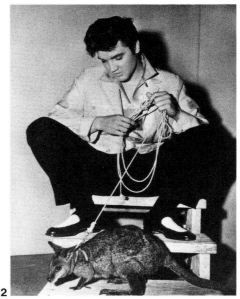

With a view to "cutting the diamond", Phillips introduced his new charge to guitarist Scotty Moore and bass player Bill Black, two musicians still in their early twenties but already "regular fixtures" of the Sun Studio. Night after night the trio assembled in the studio after knocking off from their daytime jobs, trying to create something new without really knowing what it should sound like.

After three months, Phillips' patience was all but exhausted. "We'd reached a critical point. We'd tried all sorts of things without really making any progress. I imagine Elvis must have said to himself: 'What the hell, I've nothing to lose. It's now or never!'"

It was the evening of 5 July 1954. Phillips was sitting exhausted in the control room, Moore and Black were taking a breather. Elvis picked up his guitar and started to sing with a fury that seemed to come straight from the heart. The song was a rhythm and blues number called "That's All Right", penned by Elvis's favourite songwriter Arthur Crudup. Scotty Moore and Bill Black joined in – and seconds later Sam Phillips was standing at the door. "What the hell are you playing?" he asked, bubbling with excitement. "Just don't lose the beat, and play it again!"

Within hours, the song was on tape. And on 6 July, a number was recorded for the B side: "Blue Moon of Kentucky", a laid-back bluegrass country song completely transfigured by Elvis's impassioned, electrifying interpretation. The recordings' disregard for traditional stylistic boundaries, their unorthodox blend of country and blues marked the beginning of a new chapter in popular music. At first, Scotty Moore had reservations: "When people hear this, they'll run us out of town." But Sam Phillips knew they were onto something big:

1
The first band! Elvis's earliest appearances were with lead guitarist Scotty Moore (l.) and bass player Bill Black; drummer D. J. Fontana was a later addition to the group. The trio were billed as "Elvis Presley and the Blue Moon Boys".

2
Elvis, extravagant and playful.

3
During a break between performances; for some engagements he even wore a tie.

"It hit us like a bolt of lightning. It was exactly what I had in mind for Elvis. All I had to do now was bring it to people's ears."

Next day, he took a demo to his old friend Dewey Phillips, who immediately played the record on his daily radio show. The response was overwhelming. The radio station was deluged with calls and had to play the song thirty times over. Even before the first pressing was slipped into its sleeve, shops in and around Memphis had taken 5 000 orders for the record. The landslide was starting to move. Together with Scotty Moore and Bill Black, Elvis performed at high schools and night clubs – initially without receiving a fee. If the gig did bring in the odd ten dollars, Elvis received half and Scotty and Bill a quarter each. The single climbed to No. 1 in the Memphis country and western charts and also kindled interest in Nashville and New Orleans.

But that did not mean doors everywhere were thrown open to Elvis. In the southern states, racial integration was a sensitive issue.

The depth of resentment felt towards his "nigger music" was made painfully clear to Elvis when, on 25 September, he made his first appearance at the "Grand Old Opry" in Nashville, the Mecca of country music and stronghold of die-hard "rednecks". Elvis's music made no impression on the audience. On the contrary, he was gruffly sent packing with the words: "Go back to Memphis and stick to truck driving." On the four-hour journey home, Elvis could not hold back the tears. "It hurt," he said later, "it really hurt."

But blows to his ego were few and far between. Engagements became more frequent, fees rose to the dizzy heights of 300 dollars, more singles appeared ("Good Rockin' Tonight"/"I Don't Care If The Sun Don't Shine" and "Milkcow Blues Boogie"/"You're A Heartbreaker") – and the music world's bible "Billboard" listed him eighth in the hierarchy of promising young country and western musicians. At Shreveport, Louisiana, after a concert performed before an audience of 3 500 screaming teenagers, the organizers signed him up to play every weekend for 18 months. In late '55, he managed to get out of his contractual obligations by playing a benefit concert for the YMCA. By the closing months of '54, Elvis was so busy with music that he had to give up his regular job as a truck driver with "Crown Electric".

He was on the road every day as it was. Gigs in the neighbouring states entailed endless hours of travel in Scotty Moore's Chevrolet. "Sometimes," said Elvis, "it felt as though we did nothing else but drive. We arrived in a town, did the gig, climbed back into the car and drove on. We drove and drove and drove. We even slept in the car."

With mounting engagements, professional management was urgently needed. The assignment was taken on by Bob Neal, who became Elvis's first official agent. (The job had been performed pro forma in the past by Scotty Moore). Right at the outset, Neal saw himself confronted with an unpleasant

Four photos taken from a series showing Elvis's talent for acting. Here, he is seen playing himself.

task: he had to make it clear to Scotty Moore and Bill Black (as well as the new band member, drummer D. J. Fontana) that the existing financial arrangement had to be reviewed. It was Elvis – and not the rest of the group – who pulled in the crowds, so Elvis was entitled to the lion's share of the receipts. Reluctantly, the "Blue Moon Boys" (as they'd now been christened by Neal) agreed to accept a fixed fee rather than a percentage of the take.

Neal used his influence with concert organizers and agents, spreading the net of possible venues. And although the performance schedule became increasingly tight and the pace of life little short of breakneck, Elvis kept pushing for more. "He wanted success at any price," Bob Neal recalled. "From the very beginning, he talked of becoming a film star and setting new standards. He was never satisfied with what he'd

1
Sam Phillips (l.), the owner of Sun Studios, and Elvis's first manager Bob Neal set the young singer on the road to stardom. When his success became too much for them to handle, they threw in the towel.

2
The Sun Studio facilities, proudly presented here by Sam Phillips (r.), were spartan. Nevertheless, many critics believe that this is where Elvis made his best recordings.

1

already achieved. He was impatient and constantly asked: 'What can we do to move things along a bit?'"

As for Elvis himself, he put absolutely everything he had into his work in order to realise his towering ambitions as quickly as possible. His performances became breathtaking athletic displays, his movements increasingly artistic – including splits, prostrations and pirouettes. "He put an incredible effort," said Neal, "into gaining control of the audience and getting them on his side. He responded immediately to audience reactions. And in the early days, when he was on the supporting bill, he outdid himself to make things harder for the following act."

Before long, the gruelling work bore fruit. In 1955, Elvis was hailed as the most promising country and western musician around. His income rocketed – and was immediately invested in Cadillacs (in Elvis's favourite colour pink) and a new house for his parents. He also faced his first (unsuccessful) paternity suit. The twenty-year-old singer could hardly complain of a shortage of willing admirers. Although for a time seriously dating (and even intending to marry) his childhood sweetheart Dixie Locke, Elvis was by no means impervious to female charms. In was in his nature to love being adored and idolized, and he was naturally flattered by the unambiguous offers. But when the waves of hysteria actually threatened to crash over him – and even police protection became necessary – there was no alternative but to erect external and internal barriers.

The male section of his audiences reacted to the sexual trance-like states of Elvis's female fans with growing aggression. The threats grew louder and, more than once, erupted

1, 2, 5
Elvis's first single (THAT'S ALL RIGHT MAMMA), recorded on 5 July 1954, was only a local success. But Elvis's astounding productivity in the studio led to a string of new single releases which, in the course of '55, captured the nation's attention.

3, 4
In Summer '56 – here on a Florida stage – Elvis's concerts caused a nationwide sensation. His radically new, lascivious performances earned him the nickname "Elvis the Pelvis". The mascot "Hound Dog" frequently appeared as part of the stage show.

3

4

5

into actual violence. Elvis was puzzled by the unexpected hostility. "He basked, of course, in the girls' admiration," said Bob Neal, "but he could never understand why the guys were mad at him. 'I'm no different from them,' he'd say, 'I'm just a perfectly normal guy!'"

Even if in his heart of hearts that is what he was, the "perfectly normal guy" had to learn to live in the unfamiliar, rarified air of the isolated pop star's world. And that is something he never came to terms with throughout his life.

By now, Elvis's success was so colossal that even Bob Neal, who had performed his duties as manager to the artist's full satisfaction, felt out of his depth. One evening, after another tumultuous concert on the "Louisiana Hayride" show, Neal took Elvis aside and introduced him to an oldish business-man. "Elvis, this gentleman is Colonel Tom Parker. I'm sure you two will get along just fine."

1

2

3

1 The driveway at Graceland. Built in 1939 and bought by Elvis in 1957, the mansion served as his personal refuge right up to his death.

2 Elvis loved extravagant ornamentation. The pool room at Graceland.

3 It is said that the Stutz Blackhawk, like all the other cars in Elvis's fleet, had to stand in the driveway with a full tank and keys in the ignition ready for use at all times.

4 In the park at Graceland. Two song titles are written in icing on the cake: "Hound Dog" and "Welcome Home Blues".

1 Elvis in later years with his father Vernon Presley.

2 Priscilla, Lisa Marie and Elvis Presley.

3 On 1 May 1967, Elvis Presley married Priscilla Beaulieu; the marital bliss lasted only five years.

3

When he first made his future client's acquaintance in 1955, Thomas A. Parker was 45 years old and already something of a legend in the circles in which he moved. Considering the crucial role he was to play in Elvis's career, the Colonel merits a few biographical notes. Parker was born in 1910 as the son of a travelling circus family. His parents died early, leaving Parker – with no school background whatsoever – to work in his uncle's pony circus. At seventeen he went his own way, touring the southern states with animal dressage acts, associating with showmen, circus artists and fairground callers and gaining, in those illustrious circles, something of a reputation as a foxy character.

The numerous anecdotes surrounding his life are not only entertaining to the point of being suitable film material; they also illustrate the engaging canniness of the man who made Elvis Presley the "King of Rock 'n' Roll". Here are a few of the stories people told about him:

– Parker and his travelling circus arrived in a new town. Public interest was at a low ebb and business was slack – so slack, in fact, that some of the showmen suggested lowering the admission charge from 50 to 25 cents so they would at least be spared the indignity of playing to a completely empty house. Parker had a better idea, however. Next day, a sign appeared outside the circus enclosure: "Admission: 1 dollar. 50% refund for anyone not satisfied!" And the trick worked! Everyone, of course, claimed dissatisfaction (and received 50 cents back) but the tent was full and the effective admission charge was the same.

– Parker was selling hotdogs at an annual fair. The breadrolls were long but the frankfurter inside was cut in half so it hung out the ends and looked longer than it was. If a suspicious customer checked the contents, the ends of the sausage naturally fell out. And if he then started complaining about

A pullover that made fashion history: Elvis fans know it as the "Baby I don't care pullover".

being swindled, Parker cut him short with the words: "Watch what you're doing, boy. That fine sausage of yours has just fallen on the ground. Next please!"

– Parker, now in the music business, was touring the small towns of the southern states with a country singer. In those days, it was common for country artists to perform at rodeos and livestock shows, where they enjoyed certain tax privileges. Anyone performing at other venues had to pay an entertainment levy. Parker, with a keen eye for a loophole and perfect aplomb, took a pig or a few hens along to the concerts. These he placed in a cage labelled "Livestock Show" outside the hall and thus neatly side-stepped the entertainment tax. The list of stories like these, willingly recounted by Parker and his friends, is endless. Some of the tales – such as the anecdote about him dyeing sparrows and selling them as canaries – are probably fictitious, but together they paint a picture of a man who would have sold his grandmother to the devil. They also explain why Elvis, the inexperienced country boy, accepted the man and his authority without question. The preordained paths of Parker and Presley drew closer together with the Colonel's decision (a purely honorary title, incidentally) to abandon the itinerant life and turn his attention to pastures new. To start with, he stayed in the business he knew, arranging and staging annual fairs. Then, he turned his hand to performing a similar service for music groups.

His experience with circus folk proved an asset in his new-found metier: adopting a common practice from the showman's world, he arranged for his musicians to appear twice in the same evening – in two different towns, no less! While the supporting act opened in town A, the main group stepped onstage in town B. During the break between acts, the two groups leapt into cars and drove sometimes a hundred kilometres to finish the concert in the other town. The reward: double fees for everyone.

Parker had glossy booklets about his musicians printed and sold them at the concerts (arranging for discarded copies to be collected afterwards so they could be sold again). Parker signed promotion deals with manufacturing companies (pioneering the widespread practice of "sponsoring" found in the music business today). In fact, the "poor ole Colonel", as Parker liked to call himself, was up to every trick in the book. In the space of a few years, he had the Southwest of the USA wrapped in a net of live entertainment of unparalleled size and professionalism. And he not only acted as a concert agent; he was now systematically building up his own stable of artists, who he kept permanently touring his circuit. He knew that regular bookings were still the best way to create a solid basis for a career.

His first coup as a manager was with country singer Eddy Arnold, who came onto the Colonel's books in the early forties. In 1944, he signed a recording contract for Arnold with RCA Victor and watched with satisfaction as the years of hard

Elvis was in great demand as an interviewee, but the Colonel put his foot firmly on the brake. Too many public appearances, he said, were bad for business.

Wounded but unbroken. Elvis's indomitable image made him a popular hero.

work bore fruit in the form of nationwide hits: in the late 1940s, Eddy Arnold ranked as the most successful country singer in the United States.

After Eddy Arnold (with whom he fell out in the early fifties) came the Canadian Hank Snow. Once again, life became a constant round of tours – until May '55, when on "Hank Snow's All–Stars" tour a certain Elvis Presley appeared on the bill – as a warm-up performer of course.

Presley's manager Bob Neal initially only approached the Colonel with a view to getting a few bookings. But he approached a man well-known for his sharp wits and good nose for business. The Colonel had quickly recognized young Elvis's commercial potential and wanted more than the singer's manager had in mind. Gently but firmly, Bob Neal was eased out of the saddle – in a momentous move which Neal still claims today took place with his full consent. "Elvis had become so big that I'd have had to drop everything and devote myself entirely to him. I spent a long time weighing up the pros and cons: I needed more time for my family – Elvis needed someone with no other commitments. I decided I could not be that man."

Another obstacle to Parker's ambitious plans was Sam Phillips. After his very first meeting with Elvis, Parker announced: "If he stays with Sun Records, the boy will never get anywhere." But studio boss Phillips not only had a rock-solid contract with Elvis; he could also count on Presley's unreserved loyalty. If Phillips and Bob Neal had insisted on enforcing or extending their contracts, the Colonel would probably never have managed to get his foot in the door.

But although Phillips already sensed Elvis's commercial possibilities, he largely shared Neal's view of the situation and therefore gave the Colonel the go-ahead. "I was," said Phillips, "in a tricky position. Although Sun Records was successful, I was living from hand to mouth. I couldn't get a loan because a record company at that time and in that neck of the woods was not a creditworthy enterprise. I didn't want any debts anyway. I wanted to be my own boss and carry on grooming new musicians – better to be small but independent."

Phillips authorized the Colonel to look for a recording company prepared to take over Elvis's contract with Sun Records – for hard cash naturally. Finding a buyer was no problem at all; the challenge lay in getting the right price. Columbia had made enquiries in the Spring but had withdrawn with a smile on hearing the then asking price of 18,000 dollars. Shortly afterwards, Atlantic Records bid 25,000 dollars. As Atlantic president Ahmet Ertegun later recalled: "That was absolutely all we could liquidate – and it included my desk." But the Colonel was now asking for 40,000 dollars – a sum which, in Ertegun's words, was "not only outrageous but downright preposterous" in those days.

In the end, the Colonel reached an agreement with RCA Victor. Phillips pocketed 35,000 dollars, Elvis received 5,000 dollars (as a flat–rate settlement for unpaid royalties) – and the Colonel, after gaining the confidence of Presley's parents, now had a totally free hand. He told Elvis: "You just stay talented and sexy. Leave the deals to me and we'll be as rich as rajahs." The first of those deals, the three-year contract already negotiated with RCA, was signed on 20 November 1955. The euphoria, however, was short–lived. While "Mystery Train", the last Sun single, fulfilled all expectations and gave Elvis his first No. 1 in the national country charts, the artist had problems acclimatizing in the early days at RCA.

It has to be remembered that Elvis did not write any songs himself (at most he would change the odd line), so he relied on material offered and recommended by others. Also, recording with Elvis was a long, laborious, even painful process. Back in the Sun Studio, he had often tried everyone's patience to the limit by coming into the studio completely unprepared. Long, meandering warm–up sessions and rehearsals were necessary before a polished version finally emerged.

Now, without the paternal support of Sam Phillips and under much greater pressure to succeed, Elvis found himself in a completely different ball game. The precarious situation was worsened by the fact that Phillips had pulled three talented new performers out of his hat – Johnny Cash, Jerry Lee Lewis and Carl Perkins – and with Perkins' "Blue Suede Shoes" had

ELVIS PRESLEY

landed a hit which put even Elvis's chart successes in the shade. RCA executives were so alarmed that they rang Phillips and nervously asked whether they might have spent all that money on the wrong man.

Fears were quickly dispelled, however, when Elvis walked into RCA's Nashville studios on 10 January 1956, two days after his 21st birthday, and settled down to some serious – and very concentrated – work. His old companions Scotty Moore, Bill Black and D. J. Fontana were still on board; but now they were joined by additional studio musicians (among them Chet Atkins) and a three–part vocal group consisting of Gordon Stoker from the "Jordanaires" and the brothers Ben and Brock Speer, whose "Aaaahs" and "Oooohs" were intended to take the abrasive edge off Presley's vocals.

Elvis's whole style was now noticeably different, even though only a year and a half had passed since he cut his first disc. The raw rockabilly sound was slowly being replaced by the more socially acceptable tones of the ballad; as well as the backing singers, there was also a piano filling out the formerly spartan sound and Scotty Moore's accentuated guitar was moved into the background. In fact, if it had not been for Elvis's striking mannerist voice, the result would not even have been particularly unconventional.

As with the early Sun recordings, the people involved voiced diametrically opposed opinions on the product. Gordon Stoker, a member of the "Jordanaires", had mixed feelings: "After the recordings, Elvis came over to us and said he'd really like to have us in the team for future recording sessions – provided, of course, the songs were a hit. None of us could imagine that happening, though. We weren't particularly impressed. To be honest, not long afterwards we couldn't even remember Elvis's name. For us, it was just one job among many." Sam Phillips in Memphis also found few complimentary words: "When I first heard "Heartbreak Hotel" I said: 'Those goddamn idiots are going to destroy the man.' It was a lousy recording."

Fortunately, RCA and the Colonel took a different view. Basically, they had no choice. Steve Sholes, the man responsible at RCA, knew that his head would roll if the 40,000 dollars went down the drain. And the Colonel had to pull out all the stops and make full use of all his contacts and influence to keep his horse on the right course at this crucial stage of the race. His efforts met with success. In January '56 Elvis made his first appearance on a nationwide TV show – with sensational results. The producer of "Tommy & Jimmy Dorsey's Stage Show" took up the Colonel's offer because he saw Presley as a "guitar–playing Marlon Brando". And since Brando's image as a teenage rebel was packing movie theatres throughout the country, he was hoping for a similar effect with Elvis.

He was not to be disappointed. Elvis's performance, packed with his full repertoire of hip movements, lip curls and other provocative gestures, electrified straitlaced America. The response to the broadcast was so overwhelming that the singer was signed up for five more appearances on the same show – and other broadcasting companies outbid each other to secure the "bad–ass rocker's" services in the desperate ratings war.

The Colonel suddenly found himself bombarded with offers and raised Elvis's engagement fee with relish. The Milton Berle Show was followed by the Steve Allen Show, and even Ed Sullivan, the father-figure of American TV entertainment, backtracked on earlier vows and booked Elvis for his show. Mr. Clean had sworn by all that he held sacred that this "lurch-in' urchin" with all his provocative pelvic girations would never appear on his show, but when he saw his competitors' ratings sent rocketing overnight he quickly swallowed his principles (principles which suffered the same fate eight years later when Sullivan made a similar vow regarding the Beatles). The Colonel negotiated an unprecedented fee of 50,000 dollars for three appearances – and Sullivan (who at least partly saved face by insisting that Elvis only be screened from the waist up) received the highest accolade of his TV career: 82.6 percent of networked households – a total of 54 million Americans – tuned in to the shocking live spectacle. Would Elvis have been anything at all without television? Die-hard Elvis fans would probably denounce such a question as heresy, even blasphemy. The fact is, though, that Elvis and television started their triumphant advance together. The mid-fifties saw a dramatic rise in the number of TV viewers in the United States. Once a luxury article found only in the homes of a privileged minority, the television set found its way practically overnight into the average American household (a development, incidentally, which was not seen in Europe until nearly a decade later).

Without wanting to underrate Presley's achievements, if he had appeared on the scene before the days of mass televi-sion, his fame might never have spread outside the southern states of the USA. And if he had made his debut just five, even three years before he did in fact appear, his career would probably have been considerably less glittering than it was. But history dictated otherwise. A nation of Americans sat before their recently purchased television sets and watched in stunned disbelief as the puritanical, arch-conservative world of Eisenhower, McCarthy and Billy Graham was sud-denly invaded by a subversive, lascivious element – an ele-ment which split the nation into two camps, two generations. Evangelist Billy Graham urged parents to protect their daugh-ters from Presley's corrupting influence, the all powerful women's associations mounted the barricades, and the women's magazine Cosmopolitan asked its readers (as though reviewing a man from Mars): "What is an Elvis Pres-ley?"

The clashing swords of public debate almost relegated the music to the sidelines. February '56 saw "Heartbreak Hotel"

1
22-year-old Elvis with his mother. When she died, his world collapsed.

2
Elvis the record buyer. Elvis always kept abreast of what rival artists were doing and had no scruples about singing his own versions of Little Richard or Carl Perkins songs.

3
Loud clothing and a challenging sneer – even before he stepped onstage, Elvis was a slap in the face of conservative America.

4
Elvis the performer. A decade before Beatlemania, his live appearances unleashed hysteria on a scale without precedent in the history of pop music.

5
1958: Elvis with guitarist Scotty Moore.

1

2

3

4

5

1
1956: On his first visit to New York.

2
By 1957, Elvis was appearing on stage with the vocal backing group The Jordanaires.

3
With Johnny Cash, who Sam Phillips had taken under his wing after Elvis's departure.

4
PR photos with beautiful women were approved; here a scene with Judy Tyler in JAIL-HOUSE ROCK (1957). But one thing Presley's manager watched over like a hawk: Elvis must never be seen in public with a steady girlfriend.

5
Elvis attracts the attention of television. The young singer's appearance coincided with the advent of the television set in the average American home. Without the technological revolution, the revolution in music might never have happened.

start its relentless climb to the number one spot in the pop charts and Elvis's debut LP ("Elvis Presley") – for which 362,000 advance orders were recorded in March alone – became the most successful album in RCA's history. But the headlines were grabbed by different events: the tumultuous concerts (for which the Colonel was now asking a guaranteed purse of between 15,000 and 20,000 dollars), the unbridled attempts by hysterical girls to get close to their idol at any price, a near air disaster on a flight to Nashville (which made Elvis even less fond of air travel than he already was) and finally, in March '56, Presley's first physical collapse, which he more or less shrugged off so as not to jeopardize the tour.

The Colonel, who had always argued that personal appearances and tours were essential, started to review the situation. Despite a strong police presence, he was barely able to guarantee the physical safety of his charge; Elvis's health was giving cause for concern (although the Colonel had solemnly promised Vernon and Gladys Presley that he would take extra-good care of their son in this respect) – and finally: Why take all the risks of endless, gruelling tours when a single nationwide television performance would mobilize just as many spectators (and potential record-buyers)?

From now on, Parker adopted a different strategy. Fans found fewer opportunities to see Elvis in the flesh; instead, most of his appearances were via the media. And there was one medium in particular which Elvis had long ago fixed in his sights and now it welcomed the twenty-one year-old sensation with open arms: the cinema.

Elvis
Presley

1

2

3

4

5

1
No one could accuse Elvis of being camera-shy. His behaviour in front of the camera was every bit as natural as his movements on stage.

2, 3
The first nationwide TV show with Tommy and Jimmy Dorsey on 28 January 1956 (above) gave him a national profile over-night. On 9 September, he also appeared on Ed Sullivan's show (below), where the nation's top showmaster insisted that he only be screened from the waist up so as not to cause unnecessary offence to a straitlaced America. Around 54 million viewers tuned in to the show.

4
The strenuous performances leave their mark, but the stage is the medium that suits Elvis best.

5
Another of Ed Sullivan's tricks: he seats the hip–swinging Presley at a concert piano to spare the finer feelings of sensitive viewers.

The lounging poses Elvis favoured in public brought him not only admiring glances; politicians and clergy denounced him as a threat to the morals of American youth.

A concert in Tampa, Florida, in 1956. Elvis needs the audience as much as they need him.

Elvis Presley is arrested and questioned by the Inspector of Police and his three confused detectives, the Wiere Brothers.

M-G-M presents "DOUBLE TROUBLE" In PANAVISION® and METROCOLOR

The three detectives in pursuit (the Wiere Brothers) close on Elvis Presley as he tries to make a call for help.

M-G-M presents "DOUBLE TROUBLE" In PANAVISION® and METROCOLOR

Columbia-Bavaria zeigt
ELVIS PRESLEY in *Cowboy Melodie*
Julie Adams
Jocelyn Lane
Jack Mullaney
Ein Farbfilm in Panavision®

PARAMOUNT PICTURES Presents
ELVIS PRESLEY in
PARADISE, HAWAIIAN STYLE
A Hal Wallis Production
TECHNICOLOR®   A Paramount Picture

66/80

Elvis and four good reasons why he goes girl happy during the Ft. Lauderdale vacation.

M-G-M presents "**GIRL HAPPY**" Panavision® MetroColor

© 1965 Metro-Goldwyn-Mayer Inc.   Printed in U.S.A.   7   65/64

Elvis finds himself fascinated by Shelley Fabares, the bookworm coed he is supposed to chaperone.

M-G-M presents "**GIRL HAPPY**" Panavision® MetroColor

Copyright © 1965 Metro-Goldwyn-Mayer Inc.   Printed in U.S.A.   8   65/64

Kissin' Cousins (1964)

Frankie

Kissin' Cousins (1964)

y (1966)

Harum Scarum (1965)

Kid Galahad (1962)

Follow That Dream (1962)

King Creole (1958)

Harum Scarum (1965)

Viva Las Vegas! (1964)
With Ann–Margret

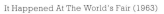
It Happened At The World's Fair (1963)

Roustabout (1964)

Viva Las Vegas! (1964)

Viva Las Vegas! (1964)

Girls! Girls! Girls! (1962)

Fun In Acapulco (1963). With Ursula Andress.

Follow That Dream (1962)

Fun In Acapulco (1963)

Follow That Dream (1962)

ollywood producer Hal Wallis (whose most notable films included "Casablanca") had been following Elvis's TV appearances and headline-grabbing career with interest. The next step seemed obvious: if young Presley had even a minimum of screen presence, there was no reason why his popularity shouldn't make cinema box-office tills ring.

In April '56 Elvis flew out to Los Angeles to take a screen test in a film studio. He passed the test with flying colours – sending movie executives scrambling (who knew how long his popularity would last?) to negotiate contracts and fees. Elvis was in seventh heaven. For him, this was a chance to realise a life-long dream. "I like to sing," he said, "but I love to act."

Presley was signed up for three films. For the first, due to be shot straight away that summer, he was paid 100,000 dollars; for the second, he received 150,000 and for the third 200,000 dollars (all of them later increased to 250,000 plus a percentage of the profits).

The Colonel's new watertight contract with Elvis, signed when the singer reached the legal age of maturity, meant that he also did well out of the deals. The details of their contract were never revealed but the basic financial arrangement was that the Colonel would initially receive a 25 percent cut of all Elvis's earnings (a cut which, from 1967 onwards, rose to 50 percent!). By now, however, Parker had abandoned all his other business interests and devoted himself entirely to Elvis. And he worked hard for his money. With dervish–like energy, he wheeled and dealed in a bid to fulfil his promise to make Elvis "as rich as a rajah":

– The Colonel persuaded RCA to release Presley's recordingsnot just once but two or three times in different combina-

Hollywood here I come! Elvis was fascinated by America's dream machine. His ultimate aim, he intimated, was a career in movies.

tions. Although music business experts described it as commercial suicide, the scheme actually worked. The public could not get enough of Elvis; they bought blind. When the single "Hound Dog" (with "Don't Be Cruel" on the B-side) was released in June '56, two million copies passed over the counter, and another two million sold shortly afterwards when "Don't Be Crue" appeared on the singles market with "Hound Dog" on the reverse. Parker turned all the rules and marketing strategies of the record business on their head.

– The Colonel turned his attention to songwriters. From now on, he decreed that anyone who wanted to write a song for Elvis (and reap handsome royalties in the process) had to agree to recognize Elvis as co-author. This particular form of sharp practice did not work all the time, however. Established songwriting teams like Leiber and Stoller rejected Parker's shady proposition out of hand. The arrangement was indeed on the verge of illegality but it brought Elvis and his manager another tidy source of income. One songwriter summed up the situation in these words: "When you deal with the Colonel, there are only two options: either you play in his team – or you don't play at all. It's their game and it's played to their rules. You get either 50 percent of what, by rights, is actually all yours – or you get 100 percent of nothing."

– The Colonel set up a fan club which, because of its vast size and almost military hierarchy, ensured a constant and reliable circle of regular customers. Its members, eligible for "special club discounts", were inundated with products and memorabilia which the Colonel either commissioned himself or allowed to be manufactured under license for a slice of the profits.

– The Colonel built up a sales network bigger and tighter than anything the pop music industry had ever seen. In 1956, there were no less than 78 Elvis articles on the market – ranging from ballpoint pens and chewing gum to dolls and perfume. By the end of 1957, total sales were estimated to be in the region of 55 million dollars; the Colonel and Elvis creamed off between 4 and 11 percent of the wholesale price of each article.

When Elvis walked onto the set to make his first Hollywood film on 22 August '56, he was a made man. Diamonds glittered on his fingers, his parents were settled in a new 40,000 dollar house in Memphis and an armada of brand new Cadillacs stood parked outside the door.

The 100,000 dollar acting fee was a pittance in comparison, but Elvis plunged into the work with enthusiasm. And the newcomer to Hollywood proved a creditable performer. The film, originally entitled "The Reno Brothers", was swiftly rechristened "Love Me Tender" and gave Elvis an opportunity to present four new songs.

Elvis was over the moon. He loved the work, he loved Hollywood, he loved – briefly but passionately – the actress Natalie Wood, he loved cruising along the boulevards in his custom-

LVIS PRESLEY

3

1
Reality and fiction come together: Hollywood lures its prey with a wad of money; a scene from IT HAPPENED AT THE WORLD'S FAIR (1963).

2
With Hollywood producer Hal Wallis Elvis signed a film contract extending over several years. The result was a total of 31 movies.

3
Key elements of Elvis's stage performances were also incorporated into the films; a scene from the film JAILHOUSE ROCK (1957).

1

1
In ROUSTABOUT (1964) with John Rick.

2
Donna Douglas touchingly attends to a prostrate, money-bedecked Elvis in the film FRANKIE AND JOHNNY (1966).

3
In his first feature film LOVE ME TENDER (1956), Elvis played alongside Richard Egan and Debra Paget.

4
With Juliet Prowse in the film G.I. BLUES (1960).

Encounters with women were many and varied in Elvis's films: JAILHOUSE ROCK (1957) (top and top right), KISSIN' COUSINS (1964) (bottom left) and ROUSTABOUT (1964).

9

ized Cadillac and winding down the window to the inevitable accompaniment of screams from teenage fans gathered on the pavement. Elvis was so deliriously happy that he toyed with the idea of settling permanently in Beverly Hills – an idea that was only abandoned because his mother steadfastly refused to leave Memphis.

When "Love Me Tender" opened on 16 November in 550 cinemas, the movie moguls were also deliriously happy. Within three days, the film recouped the million dollars it had cost to produce. The title song, released two months earlier in response to demand, attracted nearly 90,000 advance orders and helped drive Elvis fans in their thousands into the cinemas.

The only voices not raised in jubilation were those of the critics. As a performing musician, Elvis had drawn plenty of flak from uncomprehending, precocious and often cynical commentators. Now, the guardians of taste saw Elvis's first attempt at acting as a perfect target for their invective.

Accordingly, they poured buckets of scorn on the Hollywood debutant. "Is it a sausage?" asked one such critic with malicious tongue in cheek. "It's certainly smooth and slippery, but who's ever heard of a six-foot sausage? Is it a goldfish from a Walt Disney movie? Perhaps, it has the same big warm eyes, the same silky eyelashes. But who's ever seen a goldfish with sideburns? Is it a corpse? That's nearer the mark, because with its sagging lower jaw the face looks as limp and pale as Lord Byron in the waxworks museum."

The ringing of cash register bells drowned all the ugly commentaries on the sidelines. And Elvis was furiously determined to give screen performances that would make the unbeloved critics eat their words. Watching his idols James Dean, Marlon Brando and Humphrey Bogart had taught him never to laugh on screen; the most he would offer the camera was a cool smile. And when one director mentioned that he looked too plump, he crash-dieted and lost ten pounds in the next two weeks. His courteous manner was appreciated by his moviemaking colleagues but his small-town moralistic outlook made him something of an odd ball in the over-the-top world of Hollywood.

Natalie Wood later recalled that he neither relished nor understood the Californian lifestyle, endless parties and nonconformist behaviour. His idea of a great night out with his girl was a trip to his favourite restaurant for a quiet cheeseburger supper.

Although the public sex symbol behaved in private like a paragon of decency, his professional ambition remained unaffected. When it emerged that plans were being made for a film on the life of James Dean, who had died in 1955, Elvis was all ears. He wanted the role at any price, particularly since he knew Dean's films inside out.

Film producer David Weisbart, who had been involved in Dean's "Rebel Without A Cause", talked with Elvis at length

This photo has lost none of its impact through time: it conveys a sense of intimate closeness to the "King".

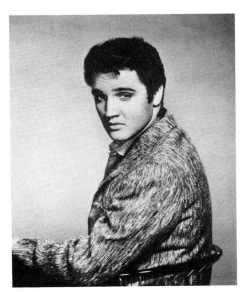

Photo from the film JAILHOUSE ROCK (1957).

Photo on Page 86:
WILD IN THE COUNTRY (1961): "An angry young man brought up without parental love rebels against the world and is suspected of murder. A great role for Elvis with five new songs." A quote from the advertising material for the film.

about the planned project and came up with an interesting assessment of the two men's characters: "Both were immature. With Jimmy (Dean), though, it was not immediately apparent because he was so withdrawn and never showed his feelings. Elvis was the exact opposite. He was open and impulsive and that made him seem emotionally much healthier. His charm lay in the very fact that he displayed his immaturity with candour. He was the personification of every teenager's dream: he was successful without having to work hard, and he had fun while still making millions."

To Elvis's boundless disappointment, the Hollywood studios decided that the film was not feasible and called an immediate halt to the project. And in the years that followed, he noted with growing bitterness that any really interesting roles mysteriously passed him by. What largely torpedoed his acting ambitions was the attitude of his manager, Colonel Tom Parker, from whom he could really have expected more support.

The Colonel must have realised at a very early stage that Elvis's meteoric rise was due to his image as a young rebel, which could not be maintained indefinitely and confined his appeal to a limited section of the public.

So the Colonel was systematically working on a shift of emphasis: the aggressive, subversive, obscene overtones of Elvis's appearances were progressively filtered out, leaving Elvis as a clean-living, well-mannered all-American boy playing the occasional Christmas carol and donating money to charity. It was no coincidence that the Colonel in those years increasingly drew Elvis's mother into the limelight. With maternal conviction, she told the world how normal, decent and god-fearing her son really was.

The first four Presley films were spared the impact of this singular transformation. Elvis played roles which at least showed him with a few rough edges: in "Love Me Tender" (1956), he was a Southerner in the Civil War who steals the wife of his brother (presumed dead); in "Loving You" (1957), he was a hot-headed, quick-tempered young musician bent on making the big time; in "Jailhouse Rock" (1957), he was an ex-convict who boxes his way to the top; and in "King Creole" (1958), he was a young man who is caught up in the seamier side of New Orleans life and actually meets and becomes emotionally involved with a hooker.

But the audience reactions to "Love Me Tender" must have given the Colonel food for thought. When the closing scene showed Elvis, shot by his brother, dying a noble hero's death, the fans in the auditorium burst into uncontrollable fits of tears and subsequently stormed the premises of the production company pleading for the distressing finale to be changed to a bloodless happy end.

Elvis never died again in any of his 31 movies. Nor did he play any more parts that were less than morally impeccable. Robert Mitchum later offered him a film in which he was to

Elvis always kept up contact with his fans and fan clubs. Here he is seen answering fan mail.

His stays in Hollywood became progressively longer; Elvis studying a film script.

88

play a bootlegger during the prohibition. The Colonel said no. Barbara Streisand offered him a part in "A Star is Born", where he would be cast in the – artistically appealing – role of a hopeless alcoholic. The Colonel said no. And in another film offer, his services were sought for the part of a cold-blooded killer. The Colonel said no. Every film script now landed first of all on the Colonel's desk, where it was carefully vetted for "wholesomeness" and "suitability for family viewing". Celluloid Elvis was no longer heard to swear nor seen to drink, he didn't lie and he didn't cheat. He became a paragon of virtue helping the poor and protecting the weak.

The Colonel was firmly convinced that, in the final analysis, what audiences wanted to see was Elvis. Scripts and dramatic devices were simply a necessary evil. Like a doll, Elvis was dressed in different costumes and allowed to play guitar and kiss pretty girls in exotic settings – always, of course, within the bounds of decency and propriety. He did it in Hawaii ("Blue Hawaii", 1961), in Acapulco ("Fun In Acapulco", 1963) and in Las Vegas ("Viva Las Vegas", 1964); he did it in a harem ("Harum Scarum", 1965), at the rodeo ("Tickle Me", 1965) and even underwater ("Easy Come, Easy Go", 1967). "Elvis films," one Hollywood producer later remarked, "don't need titles. They could be numbered."

Such criticism cut no ice with the Colonel. The money was rolling in (Elvis's income from films averaged three million dollars a year), the bothersome concerts were no longer necessary – and the Colonel had Elvis exactly where he wanted him: firmly embedded in a clean, superficial, satiated America.

But then something happened which suddenly threatened to destroy the Colonel's carefully built house of cards: Elvis received his call-up papers. Yet while the whole world mourned what was surely the end of a great career, the Colonel was rubbing his hands. He knew that a demonstration of partiotism was the very piece he needed to complete his psychological jigsaw.

His portrayal of a bold southern sharp-shooter in the film LOVE ME TENDER (1956) was perhaps not his best screen performance.

Showered with presents from fans, Elvis goes through the Christmas post.

Conflicts in Elvis's films were not allowed to be too harsh; the fans demanded a happy end – and they got it.

1
Film scene from GIRLS! GIRLS! GIRLS! (1962); Elvis as an "exotic" charmer.

2
Elvis as a patient stand-in father in IT HAPPENED AT THE WORLD'S FAIR (1963)

3
Here he sings a welcoming ballad in an attempt to ingratiate himself with Joan Black-man. Flirting with danger trying to attract the driver's attention. Scene from the film BLUE HAWAII (1961).

1
The incongruous sight of Elvis's slicked-back locks in an 18th century setting did not bother the true fans in the cinema. Elvis could have worn a wristwatch and no one would have minded.

2
Elvis never had to pack his own records like this. Nor could he, with world sales totalling more than a billion! Film scene from JAILHOUSE ROCK (1957).

3
A photo from KING CREOLE (1958).

4
Elvis Presley with Tuesday Weld in WILD IN THE COUNTRY (1961).

3

4

1
Another scene with Tuesday Weld from the film WILD IN THE COUNTRY (1961)

2
The standard of Elvis's films starts its rapid decline. Exotic settings had to be found to mask the weakness of the scripts. In HARUM SCARUM (1965), Elvis even found himself in a harem.

Photos on Page 97
Elvis with his not always helpful friends.

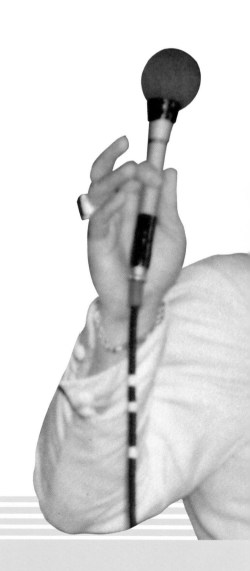

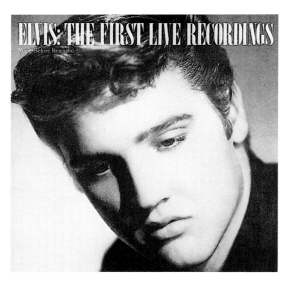

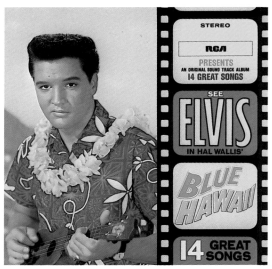

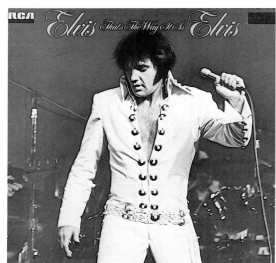

ELVIS... The Beginning Years
1954 to '56
ELVIS LIVE AT Louisiana Hayride

SONGS YOU NEVER HEARD ELVIS DO BEFORE

Also Includes 20 PAGE PHOTO BOOK

AMING STAR
Wonderful World
Night Life
All I Needed Was the Rain
Too Much Monkey Business
Yellow Rose of Texas
The Eyes of Texas
She's a Machine
Do the Vega
Tiger Man

LIVING STEREO

RCA VICTOR

ELVIS IS BACK!

50,000,000 ELVIS FANS CAN'T BE WRONG
ELVIS' GOLD RECORDS – Volume 2
A FOOL SUCH AS I
I NEED YOUR LOVE TONIGHT
WEAR MY RING AROUND YOUR NECK
DONCHA' THINK IT'S TIME
I BEG OF YOU
DON'T
A BIG HUNK O' LOVE
MY WISH CAME TRUE
ONE NIGHT
I GOT STUNG

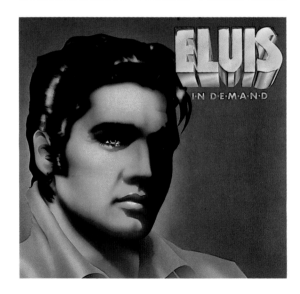

ELVIS
IN DEMAND

The King is back!

U.S. 53310761 - G.I. Presley

On 24 October 1956 Uncle Sam knocked for the first time on Elvis Presley's door. No need to panic, said the draft board, it's just a statistical survey. But when 4 January 1957 brought a medical examination showing Elvis to be in A1 condition for military service, pearls of sweat started to appear on business executives' brows.

The timing could not, in fact, have been worse. Since August '56 Elvis's singles seemed to have a season ticket for the number one spot in the American hit parade: "Don't Be Cruel"/"Hound Dog" was the national best seller for 11 weeks, "Love Me Tender" for five weeks, "Too Much" for three weeks, "All Shook Up" for eight weeks and "Teddy Bear" for seven weeks. Elvis's first film "Love Me Tender" broke all box-office records at the end of '56 and a short concert tour in Spring '57 (the last till 1970!) did the same in the world of live entertainment. Yet when "Variety" magazine officially dubbed him the "King of Rock 'n' Roll" in late '56, insiders were already muttering under their breath: For how much longer?

The musical revolution that Elvis himself had sparked brought forth a host of talented artists whose dearest wish was to step as quickly as possible into Elvis's shoes. There was Carl Perkins and Jerry Lee Lewis, Eddie Cochran and Gene Vincent, Ricky Nelson and Ritchie Valens – to name but a few of the most promising candidates. How would Elvis be able to defend his throne in the fast–moving world of music if he was put on ice for two whole years?

Elvis in Germany. He drove the jeep his senior officer used for reconnaissance patrols.

While film producers and record executives tore at their hair, the Colonel stayed cool. "An artist who is at the pinnacle of his career," he proclaimed, "should on no account appear too often in public. The fans have to be at the point where they are literally begging him for another product of his talent." Moreover, national service was just what the doctor ordered for finally cleansing Elvis's image of the "stains of the past". "They demand discipline and obedience," Elvis told a reporter, "and that's just what I aim to give them." The Colonel beamed from ear to ear.

As it turned out, however, discipline was not so high on the army's list of expectations as Elvis had assumed. The military seemed to see Elvis as a potential new Glenn Miller, a musical figurehead who would spend most of his days of service not at the front but behind a microphone.

A storm of indignation swept across the country. Veterans' associations protested against the star's preferential treatment, senators joined the fray, the case of G.I. Presley became a national political issue. Even the debate over whether he would have to lose his trademark – his decidedly unmilitary sideburns – occupied the masses and media for months.

All the uproar was totally unnecessary. The Colonel naturally insisted that Elvis should receive no special treatment; of course the hair had to go, and of course Elvis would go wherever his superiors sent him. But there would be no music! The Colonel vehemently resisted all attempts to use Elvis to promote the army's image. What he had in mind, in fact, was the reverse: he planned to use the army to promote Elvis's image.

Months of heated debate passed by before the actual date of Elvis's conscription arrived. The artist spent a comparatively quiet year in 1957 making films, taking a vacation, recording an LP of gospel songs and Christmas carols – and buying "Graceland".

In view of Elvis's growing popularity, the ranch house on Audubon Drive, Memphis – purchased just one year before – proved unsuitable. Fans and souvenir hunters besieged the house and whisked away anything they could carry. For the Presleys, there was no such thing as a private life any more and they received constant complaints from the neighbours. In March '57 Elvis found the house which measured up to his requirements and was to remain his home for the rest of his life: "Graceland". Built in 1939 and bought by Elvis for 100,000 dollars, the two-storey mansion was situated outside town and – once the necessary security systems were installed – finally provided the Presley family with the privacy they sought. After the White House, "Graceland" became the best-known residence in America.

But first came the farewells. On 20 December 1957 the long-awaited draft notice finally arrived, ordering Elvis to report for duty at the beginning of January.

Despite all the Colonel's claims to the contrary, Elvis was no normal GI – a fact which became apparent even before he set foot in the barracks.

The film company, which had already started work on "King Creole", lodged a petition for deferment on the grounds that it stood to lose 350,000 dollars. The petition was granted and Elvis was given two months' grace.

It was 24 March '58 before GI Presley, service number US 53310761, finally reported for duty at Fort Chaffee, Arkansas. The media, of course, were out in force – and the Colonel was in his element, handing out balloons with "King Creole" slogans, directing the photographers and above all making sure that full media coverage was given to the heavily symbolic hair-cutting and uniforming scenes. The general in charge subsequently said, "I think the army has demonstrated its serious intention to grant Mr. Presley no special privileges. He will be a simple soldier – just like all the other promising young men who are with us here today."

The intentions were no doubt there, but the reality was different. Photographers were certainly kept at a distance but within weeks of his call-up Elvis swapped his bunk on the base for a comfortable bungalow outside the barracks – a fact that must have given food for thought to the other "simple soldiers". Elvis had discovered a loophole in the regulations: anyone with dependants living in the vicinity was allowed to leave the barracks overnight. The rule was basically intended to cover wives and children but in Elvis's case it could be applied to his parents, who were indeed financially dependant upon him. Eight weeks after his successful demonstration of patriotism, Elvis and his parents moved into accommodation which, in terms of domestic comfort, bore a closer resemblance to Graceland than the spartan quarters of the barracks.

The family's happiness, though, was short-lived. In the early days of August, Elvis's mother's health rapidly deteriorated and she was rushed into hospital in Memphis. The diagnosis: hepatitis, complicated by excessive use of dieting pills and over-indulgence in alcohol. On 11 August Elvis was called to her sick bed; three days later, Gladys Presley was dead, a victim of heart failure at the age of 46.

Elvis was devastated. In public, barely a word crossed his lips about the woman he had loved to the point of idolatry. The pain of his loss struck him dumb, he buried his feelings deep inside. At the funeral, his only tortured exclamation was, "Everything I have is gone."

The cut was deep and the wounds healed slowly. Elvis, who had previously enjoyed his success with an unburdened heart, became taciturn and withdrawn. He probably realised himself that a stage in his life had come to an end – particularly since his longstanding companions Scotty Moore and Bill Black had also announced a parting of the ways. While Elvis was earning millions, the two musicians went home with a meagre weekly pay packet of 100 dollars (200 dollars on tours). When they voiced their dissatisfaction and demanded more money, the Colonel vetoed a raise and the musicians packed their bags.

And another thing happened which tore Elvis out of his familiar surroundings: his company was ordered to Germany. Less than six weeks after his mother's death, on 22 September, the troop carrier USS General Randall left New York port – and arrived in Bremerhaven on 1 October, where it was welcomed by 500 teenagers.

While Elvis – accompanied by his father, his grandmother and a small group of friends from Memphis – settled down in Bad Nauheim for a 17 month tour of duty, those who were left behind in America pondered the problem of how to keep the ball rolling in a world without Elvis. Nearly all his existing recordings had already been released and new recordings were out of the question during his period of military service. So old wine was poured into new bottles. Chartbusting material was mixed with less well-known recordings and released

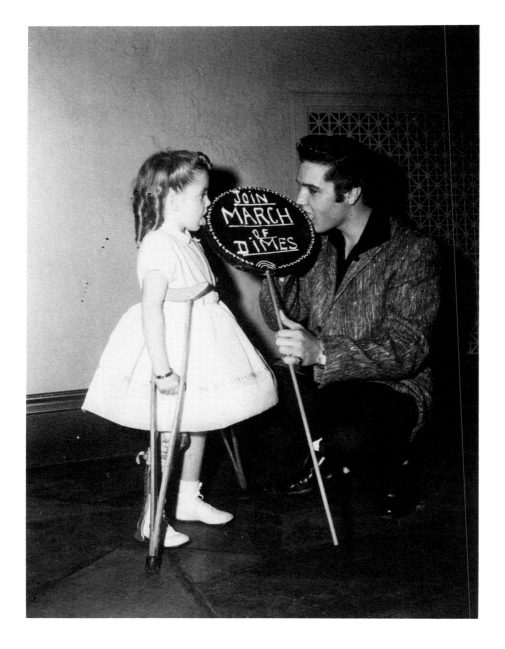

Promotion work for charity: Elvis supports an aid fund for physically handicapped children.

in various combinations. At the same time, the Colonel devoted himself to producing contrived snippets of news aimed at keeping the press happy and maintaining Elvis's popularity at fever pitch. "I consider it my patriotic duty," he announced, "to keep Elvis above the 90 percent mark in the tax progression." He reported that Elvis's income in 1958 amounted to two million dollars and in 1959, he said, it would be even better. His optimism certainly seemed well–founded. An average of 10,000 fan letters a week – more than ever before – arrived in Bad Nauheim, and re-released records were snapped up as though they were the star's last vital spark. As the Colonel predicted, Elvis's absence acted like an appeal to the fans to remain loyal to their King.

Meanwhile, Elvis sat behind the wheel of a jeep and drove through the Taunus. His conduct in the army gave absolutely no cause for complaint. In the words of a military spokesman: "He sits with his buddies in the snow and eats the same chow. They see he's a perfectly normal guy and they all stand by him."

His diligent attention to duty even earned him promotion in the military hierarchy. As a sergeant, he now took home an imposing $ 135.30 a month – enough to cover about 15 percent of the rent he paid for the villa at Goethestrasse 14 in Bad Nauheim.

Behind the front door of the Presley residence (with its sign announcing "Autograph hour from 19.30 to 20.30" to keep overly persistent visitors at bay), life was not quite so military. Elvis's closest friends were constantly at hand and he had no cause to complain about a lack of female visitors. A fleeting romance with the actress Vera Tshechowa was alleged – and during a period of leave in Paris his room waiter reported that "the most beautiful women laid their hands on his door handle." Years later, in fact, photos were published which Colonel Parker would have prefered not to see: Elvis on a visit to Munich in the intimate company of strippers and ladies of even worse repute.

But there were two women, in particular, worth mentioning: Elvis's father Vernon met his future (second) wife Dee Elliot in Frankfurt, and Elvis made the acquaintance, on 18 September '58, of Priscilla Beaulieu, the fourteen-year-old daughter of a US captain. Elvis was immediately fascinated by the girl, who showed no sign of being impressed by the name Presley. During the remaining months of his national service, the couple met several times and, on his departure from Germany in early March 1960 Elvis gave a firm promise that they would see each other again soon.

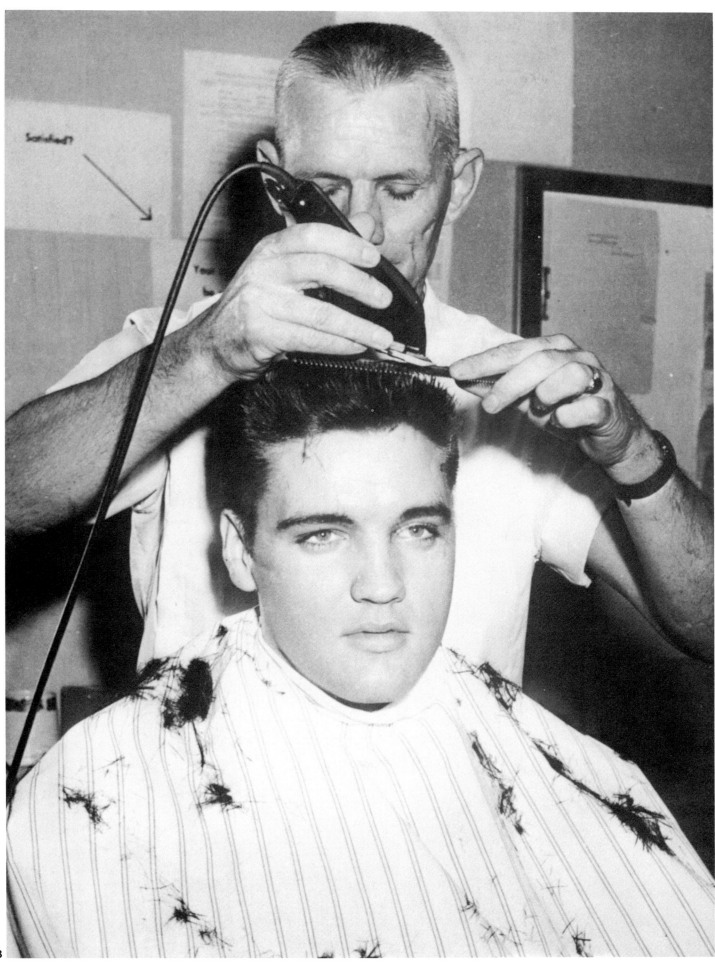

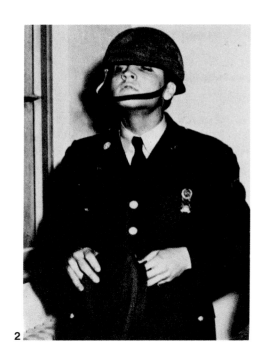

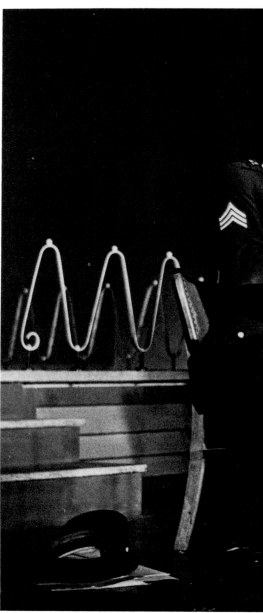

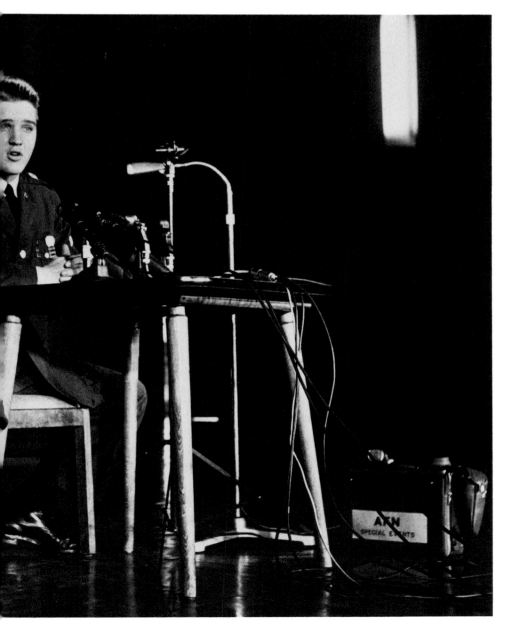

1
On 14 August 1958 Gladys Presley died.
Elvis and his father Vernon waiting at the
hospital for the medical bulletin.

2
The helmet fits! Elvis trying on his uniform
in the changing room.

3
The strain of military service can be clearly
seen in the face of the new recruit.

4, 5
Those who feared that Elvis would vanish
from the public eye during his time in the
army found themselves proved wrong. On
the contrary, Elvis's demonstrative display
of patriotism made the former rebel admi-
rably acceptable to the Establishment.

On 5 March 1960, the world had Elvis back. The train from New York to Memphis was rocked by waves of delight as though he had never been away. In Memphis itself, the traffic chaos was so bad that the police had to escort him to Graceland. There, the Colonel was already waiting with a packed work schedule for the returning star. Within two weeks of his arrival, Elvis was ushered into the studio at Nashville to start freshening up the Presley record archives. RCA didn't want to wait a day longer than necessary. The forthcoming single already had an order number and 1,275,077 orders were reported in the shops – and there was still nothing on tape! In a single night-time session, Elvis produced six new songs (his first in stereo), including the single "Stuck On You", which surprised no one by topping the hit parade four weeks later. The very next day, he set off for Miami to rehearse for the "Frank Sinatra–Timex Show". Although Sinatra's derogatory comments about rock and roll ("the music of largely feeble-minded cretins") had made him few friends among fans, the Colonel saw the TV spectacular as an ideal vehicle for catapulting his "boy" into the limelight with a bang. For a new record fee of 125,000 dollars, Elvis made a brief appearance in the show, where he was forced into a tuxedo and made to sing a duet with his host, the ultimate establishment figure: while Sinatra gave a rendering of Presley's "Love Me Tender", Elvis had to return the compliment by singing Sinatra's hit "Witchcraft".

Although the ratings were just what the Colonel had hoped, Elvis's fans, after months "in the desert", had expected something different. Was this the same man they had taken into their hearts four years ago? Was this the man who not only revolutionized music but also voiced the rebellious feelings of an entire generation? The signs that were witnessed before his conscription but not generally taken to herald a change of direction were now unmistakable: Elvis was no longer wild, he was alarmingly tame; still as talented as ever, of course, but with no sign of the old fire.

On 26 April, Hollywood came back into Elvis's life. Producer Hal Wallis was so impatient that he had already had parts of the film "G.I. Blues" produced in Germany. His belief that

Photo on Page 112:
The return! In March 1960 Elvis (accompanied by the Colonel) returned to America and was given a tumultuous reception. Making an appearance on the Frank Sinatra-Timex Show, he staged his comeback on American television.

"Elvis films are the only safe bet in show business" was once again confirmed, but when the film was released it too left a stale aftertaste. The script, based on Elvis's time in the army, was too thin, the characters too transparent and the soundtrack too insipid. Even Elvis was so disappointed with the result that, in a rare moment of criticism, he asked the Colonel to apply stricter standards when selecting future scripts.

His words had the opposite effect, however. Box office receipts seemed to confirm the concept of the lightweight screenplay. And as the Colonel saw dollars as the only measure of success, the formula was repeated ad nauseam. No problems, no social criticism, no controversial themes – "See Elvis where the fun never stops" read the advertising blurb on the billboards for one of his films. Elvis was desperately unhappy about most of his roles and, during shooting, went out of his way to show his lack of interest. When it came to the crunch, however, he invariably bowed to the Colonel's decision to continue churning out the endless stream of trash.

Many people have wondered why a grown man with a mind of his own should have displayed such blind obedience. Record producer Phil Spector, himself an ardent Elvis fan, even contended that the Colonel kept Elvis loyal through hypnosis. As preposterous as Spector's suggestion most certainly is, Elvis's behaviour in those years did seem to bear it out.

If the films were bad, the effect on Elvis's music was devastating. Right up to the end of the sixties, he never set foot on a concert stage – and his record releases, mostly film songs, were generally nothing but obvious vehicles for promoting the endless string of Hollywood products.

The way those film songs were produced casts a telling light on the stagnant routine which had crept into Presley's record productions: his music publishers would send out the film scripts to a handful of potential authors, with crosses marking the places where songs were needed. Demo recordings of all the submitted songs were then played in the studio. If Elvis disliked a particular song, it was discarded immediately; if he was unsure, the decision was taken after two or three plays; if a title met with his approval, the entire band listened to the demo a few more times and then – usually without changing the arrangement – got straight down to recording.

This conveyor belt method of production took its toll on the quality of the product. From 1963 to 1968, Elvis had no chart-topping hits, and in the country and rhythm & blues charts, where he made his first big breakthrough, his name did not appear at all. His waning musical stature, of course, was also due to other factors: Bob Dylan, the Beatles and the Rolling Stones had appeared on the pop music scene, artists who on grounds of age alone were better qualified for the role of teenage idol than a now plumpish Elvis Presley in his mid-thirties. They wrote their own, personalized songs, protested against Vietnam, smoked marihuana, created new fashions and made Elvis look like a diamond-studded fossil. Elvis was

1

1
Elvis with Frank Sinatra. The appearance drew fire from many of the viewing public because, in rock 'n' roll circles, Sinatra was decried as a reactionary.

2, 3, 4
Back at Graceland. Elvis spent the rest of his life barricaded behind the gates that were installed to protect him from over-persistent fans.

ELVIS·PRESLEY

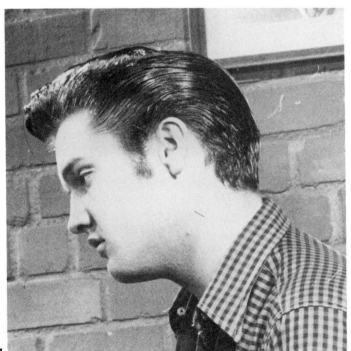

crowded off the stage and – until his rebellion against the Colonel in '68 – dejectedly withdrew into private life.

Much of his now ample free time was spent remodelling Graceland. Back in 1957, in the first six months after he bought the house, he invested 500,000 dollars in modernising and furnishing his new home. But the refurbishment was not to end there. Elvis now ordered extensions, conversions, revisions and reappointments – creating a bizarre jumble of styles which even today draws gasps of incredulity from visitors.

What many would dismiss as out-and-out kitsch is explained partly by Elvis's small-town background and partly by an uncompromising taste in design. He would quite happily give one room a rococo air with lots of gold and crystal while right next door lay the "jungle room" steeped in tropical Polynesian atmosphere.

The business of keeping body and soul together was taken seriously at Graceland. A 31-item shopping list ensured that at least the "bare necessities" were kept in the house at all times. These ranged from fresh ground meat to sauerkraut, from shredded coconut to banana pudding (to be made each night), from peanut butter to diet pills. (For short excursions, such as visits to the cinema, there was an abbreviated list of provisions running to 15 items.)

Elvis, especially in his later years, loved eating. He would devour huge quantities of cheeseburgers, peanut butter sandwiches, pizzas, melons and ice cream – preferably at night. This not exactly being the best way to keep a trim figure, his weight increased from just under 80 to more than 120 kilos.

Hereditary predisposition (on his mother's side) may have played a role here; career frustration was certainly a factor, and sheer boredom no doubt did the rest. The "King" was a prisoner in a gilded cage, unable to lead a normal life outside Graceland.

Neal Matthews, a member of Elvis's vocal group "The Jordanaires", saw the signs at an early stage: "He could only go out at night. Once, I asked him if he fancied a round of golf. 'You bet I do,' he said, 'but I can't.' If he'd gone onto the golf course, the whole neighbourhood would have turned out. He was just bound to be unhappy in that situation."

Elvis tried to escape from his isolation, at least temporarily, by arranging night-time extravaganzas. He would rent a cinema, a roller-skating rink or – for a special treat – an entire amusement park. The Memphis authorities turned a blind eye when the city's most celebrated son and his entourage ran the roller coaster beyond the safety limit till the early hours of the morning. Invitations went out to everyone in Elvis's circle of acquaintances, especially, of course, the "Memphis Mafia", the cluster of sworn friends and lackeys that steadily grew around Elvis over the years. Bodyguards, chauffeurs, a cook, a hairdresser, later even a karate instructor and a personal physician, plus a sprinkling of court jesters whose only

To escape from his isolation, Elvis would rent whole cinemas and amusement parks (r.) at night so that he could let off steam with his friends. Here he is seen with his girlfriend at the time, Anita Wood.

function was to keep the "King" in good humour. Elvis was the meal ticket for them all. And he not only paid them a regular salary but also showered them with princely gifts.

The "happies", as Elvis called them, were more often than not brand new Cadillacs. He bought over a hundred of them in the course of his life – for himself (although he was occasionally unfaithful to his favourite automobile, flirting instead with Mercedes, Rolls Royce and Ferrari), for members of the "Mafia" and even for complete strangers. One evening, so the story goes, he decided to buy two new models from his Cadillac dealer. Outside the shop, he saw an evidently not so well-heeled young couple gazing in awe at the fabulously priced limousines. He spoke to them, invited them to pick out the model they liked most and, without saying another word, paid for it with a cheque.

Elvis spent money with both hands. Unlike his discoverer Sam Phillips (who invested in the burgeoning Holiday Inn chain and made a fortune), Elvis was only interested in liquid assets; he wanted money at his fingertips. Stock investment and market speculation were not his scene. He gave away thousand dollar bills, handed out diamonds, made presents of houses. He even gave Sammy Davis Jr. a 30,000 dollar ring because, as Elvis put it, "nobody thinks of giving a rich man anything."

Although he was genuinely adored by the vast majority of his retinue, his generosity no doubt helped deepen their attachment. There was even a mysterious symbol intended as the seal and badge of their fraternal friendship: TCB – "Taking Care of Business (in a Flash)" – became the latter-day Elvis's creed, his code of honour, his pragmatic philosophy. He wore the three letters emblazoned on a heavy diamond ring, he immortalized the emblem in 1975 by having it painted on the tail of his private jet and he presented the members of his inner circle with "TCB" badges and pendants in every conceivable design.

The presence of a woman in the all-male coterie around Elvis was hard to imagine. But the day did dawn. Elvis, keeping his earlier promise, invited Priscilla Beaulieu to Graceland, where in May '62 the sixteen-year-old took up permanent residence.

Elvis's principal desire at first – he was 11 years the girl's senior – was probably confined to completing Priscilla's education. He sent her to school, advised her on make-up and helped her select her wardrobe. But paternal support quickly changed into almost neurotic authority. Just as he impressed his stamp on music – in the early years at least – and imposed his own style on Graceland and everyone who frequented it, so he moulded the girl who was to become his wife. The King created a queen in his own image.

Priscilla's freedom to look and behave as she wished was increasingly curtailed. She couldn't even eat her favourite food – tuna salad – because Elvis hated the smell. When Elvis

Inside Graceland. In the background, the piano room where Elvis liked to spend time alone.

had a much-publicized affair in Hollywood with the actress Ann-Margret, Priscilla dressed and wore her hair exactly like her rival just to please her future husband. And when they married in Las Vegas on 1 May 1967, there was even a certain facial resemblance between Elvis and "his creation".

The marriage (which even received the Colonel's blessing, though he would really have preferred Elvis to stay single) lasted less than six-and-a-half years. But its issue, daughter Lisa Marie, born exactly nine months after the wedding, radically changed Elvis's life. His new responsibility played a significant role in shaking him out of his lethargy. He "rebelled" – for the first time in his life – against the Colonel and insisted on returning to where he had always belonged: the stage.

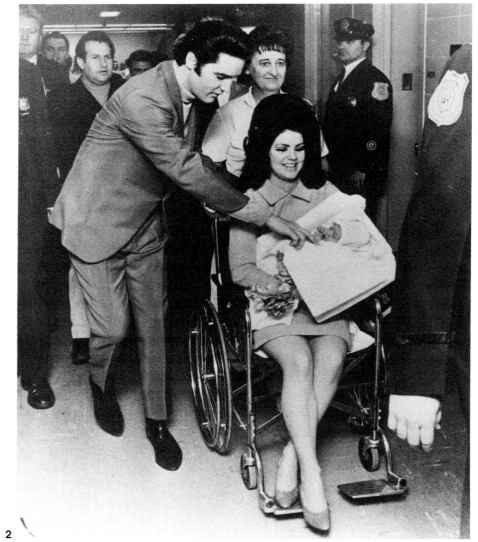

1
Wedding in Las Vegas. On 1 May 1967 Elvis led Priscilla Beaulieu, who he had met eight years earlier in Germany, to the altar.

2
Exactly nine months after the wedding, on 1 February 1968, Lisa Marie Presley was born. On her 25th birthday in 1993, she will inherit the Presley estate.

Photo on Page 121 (centre):
Elvis Presley's private jet, named after his daughter Lisa Marie.

GRACELAND TOURS

NO REFUNDS

TIME

GRAC

382

NO RAINCHECKS

LAND

860

ELVIS
AARON
PRESLEY

JANUARY 8, 1935
AUGUST 16, 1977

SON OF

VERNON ELVIS PRESLEY
AND
GLADYS LOVE PRESLEY

FATHER

LISA MARIE PRESLEY

WAS A PRECIOUS GIFT FROM GOD
CHERISHED AND LOVED DEARLY
HAD A GOD-GIVEN TALENT THAT HE SHAR
IN THE WORLD, AND WITHOUT A DOUBT
BECAME MOST WIDELY ACCLAIMED;
RING THE HEARTS OF YOUNG AND OLD
AS ADMIRED NOT ONLY AS AN ENTERTA
THE GREAT HUMANITARIAN THAT HE
IS GENEROSITY AND HIS KIND FEELING

The Comeback

"If any more movie contracts are signed, I will not turn up for filming." The finality of that decision, announced by Elvis in an uncharacteristically sharp tone, was unmistakable. But the Colonel was himself fully aware that the Hollywood card had already been hopelessly overplayed. Receipts from the last few films were so disappointing that the Hollywood studios refused to carry on paying Elvis his previously guaranteed fee of one million dollars (or more). A drop in price, in the Colonel's eyes, was entirely out of the question; for a brand product like Elvis, there would be no discounts or special offers, even in times of crisis.

In early '68, he came up with a deal negotiated with the television broadcasting company NBC: 500,000 dollars for a TV special – plus 500,000 dollars for a television film to be screened at a future date. Elvis had his way, the Colonel had his million.

But the Colonel would not have been the Colonel if he had not had his own clear-cut ideas about the kind of show the TV special should be. Since the programme was to be broadcast in the run-up to Christmas, he wanted Elvis to sing a collection of popular carols and to finish the show with a courteous Christmas message to the viewers. Steve Binder, the show's producer, was horrified: "It was perfectly clear to me that this programme was the moment of truth for Elvis. If he'd made another of those unspeakable MGM or Paramount films, his career would be in the can. He would have been remembered as the phenomenon that appeared in the fifties, wiggled

Photo on Page 126 (bottom):
The Elvis Presley Memorial Chapel in Tupelo, Mississippi. It was consecrated on 17 August 1979.

his hips and had a brilliant manager. On the other hand, if he could prove in this special that he was still the No. 1, he'd be able to shake off the whole patina at a stroke."

To hammer home the seriousness of the situation, Binder persuaded a vacillating Elvis to join him in an unusual experiment: at four o'clock in the afternoon, they walked together down Los Angeles' busy Sunset Boulevard to put Elvis's grass-roots appeal to the test. In former times, they would have been mobbed within minutes, but now there was no reaction. Passers-by continued on their way, either because they failed to recognize the star in their midst or because they thought he was just another of the numerous Elvis clones who now walked the streets.

Binder succeeded in steering Elvis towards a confrontation with the Colonel. As a result, the idea of turning the special into a family Christmas show was quickly dumped, although the Colonel still insisted that the programme should at least close with a carol.

Binder remained adamant, so did the Colonel. Finally, one evening, it came to a showdown. As Binder reports, "Elvis was present at the meeting, his head bowed forward. The Colonel was furious: 'Elvis himself wants to sing this carol – don't you, Elvis?' Elvis just nodded. But when the Colonel left the room, he looked up and said: 'Okay, we'll take it out.'" On 27 June '68,

129

Priscilla (r.), Vernon Presley and his second wife celebrate Elvis's return to the stage on 30 July in Las Vegas.

in front of a studio audience, the first of four segments of the show was recorded. Elvis was nervous, even trembling. "I haven't stood in front of an audience for seven years. What'll I do if they laugh at me?"

Nothing could have been farther from the audience's mind. At long last they were seeing the Elvis they had so sorely missed for nearly a decade. He'd shed a good bit of weight, the side-burns were back and he was wearing a black leather suit which seemed to conjure up all the animal passion of his younger years. (This was another battle the Colonel had lost: Elvis rejected his proposal of a gold showbiz suit in favour of Binder's preference for a black leather outfit – actually the trademark, at the time, of the singer Gene Vincent!)

And there was another point on which the Colonel had to concede defeat: instead of the closing carol, Binder had commissioned a song which was to set the points for Elvis's future career. It was called "If I Can Dream" and described a dream of a more humane society – a subject which had never before figured in Elvis's repertoire. While the Colonel grumbled "Only over my dead body", Elvis bubbled with enthusiasm and soon came up with a stage presentation.

When the programme was screened on 3 December 1968, America responded with rapturous applause. The critic John Landau, now Bruce Springsteen's manager, wrote: "It was a magical moment, seeing a man who had been lost and had now found the way back home. Although most of the songs were ten or twelve years old, he played them as though they had just been written."

Elvis, too, intoxicated by the success he had so long been denied, was moved to great words: "I intend to make a lot of changes. You just can't go on doing the same thing year after year. I don't plan to continue making three films a year. I miss

The smiles are a smokescreen. The marriage between Elvis and Priscilla was a farce from the outset. On 23 February 1973, she asked him for a divorce.

the contact with the public and I'm going to get back on the stage very soon."

But first he returned to the studio. In January '69, he started a recording session in Memphis which was to be the most productive of his entire career. This was not Elvis going through the motions playing uninspiring movie songs; it was Elvis at long last singing again with heart and soul. 36 new titles were hammered out in the space of a few days, titles which included classics like "In The Ghetto" and "Suspicious Minds", which on 4 November '69 once again took Elvis to the No. 1 slot in the American hit parade. More important to Elvis, though, was his return to the stage. Instead of setting up a conventional tour, the Colonel sent him to the super-ritzy, newly opened "International" hotel in Las Vegas. The four-week engagement paid the neat round sum so dearly loved by the Colonel (a million dollars), but Elvis was not interested in the financial side: "I don't care whether I make any money out of it or not. The main thing is to give the people a good show."

And he certainly did that. He rounded up the best and most expensive studio musicians in the business, rehearsed – with orchestral backing – over a hundred songs and finally

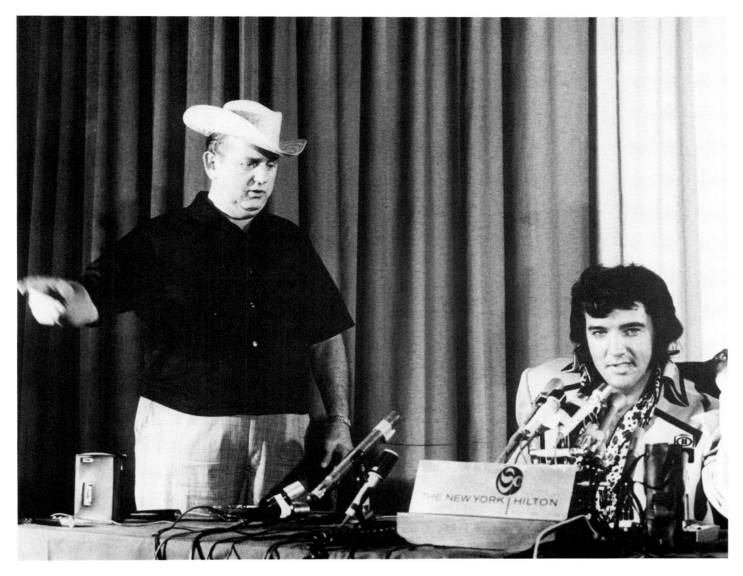

His private life is a disaster but his career never looked in better shape. Together with the Colonel, he announces new plans at a press conference in the New York Hilton.

packed every ounce of his pent-up frustration into the performance. "For nine years," he said after one of the concerts, "I wanted to get back on the stage. In the last few years, the pressure became so intense that I couldn't have stood it much longer. A concert like this tonight gives me more than all the film songs of my career put together."

The shows in Las Vegas were such an overwhelming success that Elvis was signed up for another month of concerts just half a year later. And he returned with a very different repertoire. In the first series of shows he mainly performed old hits; this time the material was more modern, more audacious, even including the odd cover version of new hits ("Proud Mary").

A month later, in February '70, the Colonel offered the next Elvis extravaganza. At the Astrodome in Houston (capacity: 44 500 seats) Elvis played six concerts to a total audience of a quarter of a million people. His fee: 1.2 million dollars. "My boy," the Colonel dryly remarked, "needs these big venues in order to do justice to his image as the "King". Las Vegas and the Astrodome are in exactly the right price category."

But Elvis wanted more than just a few spectacular gigs. During the remaining years of his life, he pushed himself to the limit –

133

with no regard for his health – in a bid to catch up on all the things he had so sorely missed in the sixties. On 9 September – after a hiatus of 13 years! – he embarked on his first concert tour, a tour which was to be followed by countless others in the course of the next seven years.

He also made more films, but not in Hollywood. Camera teams accompanied Elvis on two of his tours and documented a phase which – apart from the stormy days of '56/'57 – was probably the hardest but happiest time of his life. "That's The Way It Is" (1970) and "Elvis On Tour" (1973) showed the King in full possession of his musical faculties, blessed with a voice which never let him down even after weeks on tour. He was accompanied by a string of fine musicians, notably James Burton (lead guitar), Jerry Scheff (bass) and Ron Tut (drums), who furnished him with backing rhythms that made him the envy of every performer in the business.

Although Elvis was on stage for nearly six months of the year, his performances never became routine. He devoted his full attention to every concert and gave his best to every audience. With improvisations and song selections, he came up with constant surprises for musicians and spectators alike.

Nevertheless, his show developed into a ceremony with an almost ritualistic framework. There was the band's dramatic opening with "Also sprach Zarathustra", there were the sweat-stained handkerchiefs and scarves which Elvis threw to the fans from the stage and there were the words repeated after every concert: "Elvis has left the building."

Tour followed tour, interrupted only by lengthy engagements in Las Vegas and a number of extravaganzas (bringing in prodigious sums), which were of course particularly dear to the Colonel's heart. In June '72, Elvis played to capacity crowds at four shows staged in New York's Madison Square Garden (his fee: 750,000 dollars); the mammoth concert at the Silver Dome in Pontiac, Michigan attracted 80,000 spectators and earned Elvis 816,000 dollars; and finally, on 14 January '73, the Colonel set up his most ambitious project ever: under the title "Aloha From Hawaii", Elvis's performance in Honolulu was broadcast via satellite to every continent. Estimated audience: one billion people!

Back home in Memphis, though, things did not look so rosy. Priscilla Presley was bored to death. Even when her busy husband was in residence at Graceland, their paths rarely crossed. Elvis was a night owl who only went to bed after sunrise, whereas Priscilla got up early to go riding or practice karate. Elvis's inevitable affairs made matters worse – and when Priscilla herself finally fell for another man, the karate instructor Mike Stone, it was only a question of time before the couple went their separate ways. When Priscilla knocked on Elvis's hotel room door in Las Vegas on 23 February '73 and asked him to grant her a divorce, Elvis – once again – felt his world collapse around him. His dreams and flights of fantasy at the first climax of his career had been shattered by the sud-

On stage, Elvis is as fascinating as in the early days of his career. The constant tours, however, coupled with an amphetamine habit running out of control, take a rapid toll on his health.

den death of his mother; now he had lost a woman whose love – despite his own culpable conduct – he had always felt he could depend on.

Elvis was livid, beside himself with rage, a Mephistophelean figure spitting out wild threats against the rival lover – and when his fury was spent, all that remained was an empty, despondent man. On 15 October '73, a week after the official separation, Elvis was taken to hospital for the first of many courses of treatment.

The break-up of the marriage was not the real reason for Elvis's physical decline, however. The gruelling tours took their toll on his health, and that toll became heavier as Elvis increasingly resorted to "medication" to help him cope with the superhuman demands of his work. Amphetamines, prescribed by a doctor, but lethal in the quantities Elvis was taking, wasted his body despite his increased weight. For the

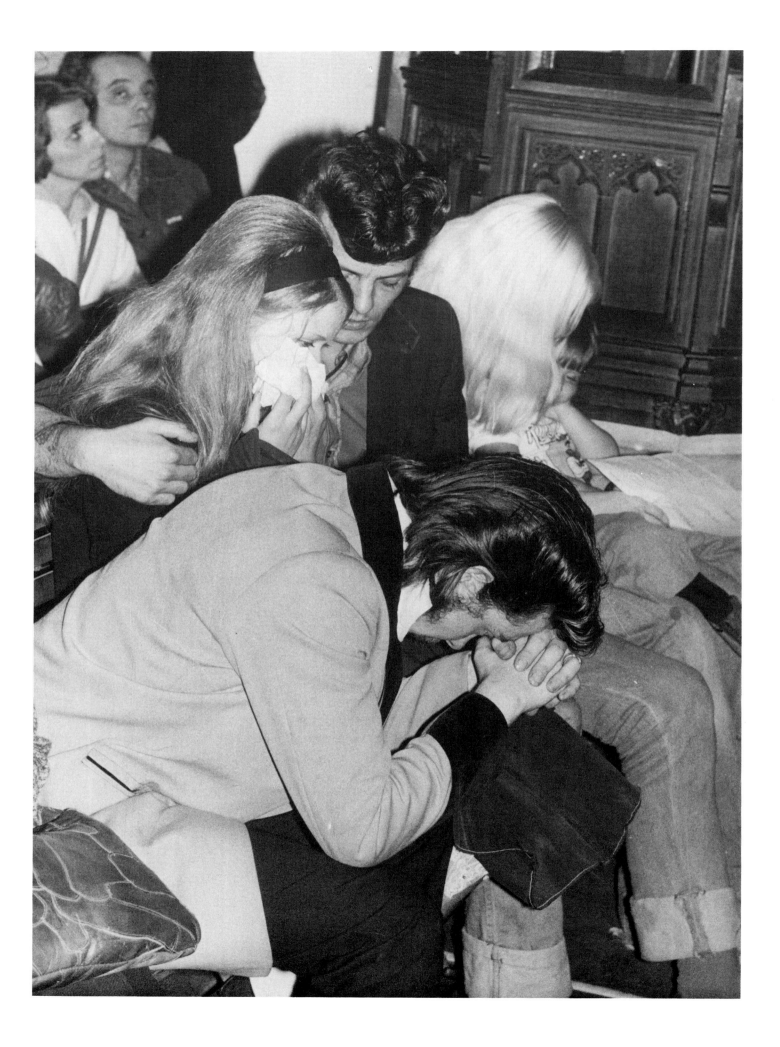

rest of his life, tours and periods of hospitalization alternated with horrifying regularity.

There were plenty of warning voices but no one felt they could actually tell Elvis to change his ways. Shouldn't the Colonel have put his foot down? Certainly, but he was now living in far-off Palm Springs and had little contact with Elvis other than by telephone. Anyway, he had no desire to interfere with Elvis's private life. What about Elvis's friends in the "Mafia"? They were also, of course, culpably negligent, but how many of those slavish yes–men could have found the courage to stand up and tell the "lord and master" how to run his life?

It is possible that even if those around him had taken a tougher line, their efforts would have been in vain. Elvis was "hooked" on tours; concerts had become an all-consuming passion. Now that his private life was a fiasco there was nothing, perhaps, to keep him at home.

On 17 August '77 another tour was scheduled to begin. As always in the days before the opening concert, Elvis was nervous and irritable. But this time he had another reason to feel vexed: under the title "Elvis – What happened?", three former members of the "Mafia" (one of them his childhood friend Red West) had just published a book on Elvis containing sensational inside information on life behind the scenes. The authors claimed they wrote the book to give Elvis a jolt and halt his progress down the road to self-destruction. Their real motives, however, were palpably obvious (all three left Elvis's service against their will). Elvis had every reason to be indignant and bitter.

On the evening of 15 August, at 10.30 precisely, Elvis, accompanied by his bodyguards, drove to his dentist for some last-minute treatment before the start of the impending tour. At 1.30 a.m. the party returned to Graceland. Elvis then spent the night with a small group of friends. Among them was twenty-year-old beauty queen Ginger Alden, Elvis's girlfriend of several weeks standing. When she went to bed around 9 a.m. Elvis said he wanted to read a little. When she got up at 2 p.m. she found his lifeless body in the bathroom. All attempts at resuscitation proved futile. Even at the hospital, the doctors were powerless to help. At 3.30p.m., on 16 August 1977, the "King" was declared dead.

Elvis had left the building.

Photo on Page 136:
The news of his death on 16 August 1977 spread around the world like wildfire. Fans everywhere, like those here in London, mourned the passing of their King.

Taking Care of Elvis

The grave in Memphis has become a place of pilgrimage. At the same time, the souvenir industry has grown to incredible proportions.

The news of Elvis's death spread like wildfire around the globe. When his remains were laid out at Graceland the following day, 30,000 tearful mourners turned up within hours to file past the coffin. The funeral itself was attended by 100,000 people, who flocked from all over the United States to pay their final respects to the "King". His remains were buried at the Forest Hill Cemetery alongside the grave of his mother, but a few weeks later fear of grave robbers prompted a decision to transfer the two graves to the garden at Graceland (which also became the final resting place of Elvis's father, who outlived his son by two years).

The results of the autopsy were never revealed, which fuelled the wild rumours surrounding his death all the more. Had Elvis been pumping himself full of more than just amphetamines? Were there other, harder drugs involved, drugs he had always vehemently denied taking? Did he have bone cancer and was that the reason he took such vast doses of drugs? Was it the knowledge of his illness that drove him to embark on those endless tours, so that he could reach as many fans as possible before he died? Such speculation (in-

139

cluding ludicrous rumours such as the one that Elvis was alive and had been seen behind the wheel of a Cadillac in Memphis) kept the Elvis cult at boiling point.

And, of course, there was the dynamo of economic interest. In the twelve months following Elvis's death, sales of his records soared to a level matched only by the turnover figures at the peak of his career. Even today, more than ten years on, "new" LPs are regularly launched and snapped up by a circle of devoted fans, boosting the 1.4 billion dollars which Elvis's records have brought in to date. The souvenir industry is doing a roaring trade. "Elvis business" (started by the Colonel, taken over by Vernon Presley, now in the hands of the Elvis Presley Estate and due to be transferred to Elvis's daughter Lisa Marie on her 25th birthday in 1993) is flourishing more than ever. 83 manufacturers are producing articles which have little or nothing to do with Elvis – from "Love Me Tender" shampoo through soft "Elvis Hound Dogs" for children to "Elvis Wine", which the advertiser tells us: "Elvis would have drunk if he'd been a wine-drinker." Requests for licences to use his name have to be truly perverse to fall on deaf ears among the administrators of Elvis's estate (dustbin and lawn sprinkler manufacturers, for example, have had their petitions rejected). In 1986, "Elvis memorial industry" sales totalled 50 million dollars.

The Elvis museums also still draw the crowds – especially Graceland, which was opened to the public on 7 June '82 and attracts over half a million visitors a year, who hand over $ 11.95 a head for

the privilege of casting an eye over Elvis's wonderful world. There are also museums in Tupelo (the house where he was born); Nashville; Orlando, Florida; Gatlinburg, Tennessee; and Woodbridge, Virginia. Other memorials are planned in Hollywood and Honolulu, and a "Heartbreak Hotel" is to be erected alongside Graceland.

But the biggest museum – after Graceland – is on wheels, 54 wheels to be exact. With a fleet of gigantic articulated trucks, former Elvis confidant Jimmy Velvet tours the United States, keeping alive Elvis's memory by presenting his collection of treasures – for an admission fee of course – to fans in the remotest corners of the country. (Apart from costumes and other personal items, he owns 13 of Elvis's fleet of cars).

Most of the credit for keeping alive the "King's" memory, however, must surely go to his fans and the worldwide network of fan clubs still in existence today. In 1987, in the week of the tenth anniversary of his death, 50,000 die-hard Elvis admirers made a pilgrimage to Graceland to stand in silence at the graveside of "their King". (The English fan club even received special permission to land at Memphis airport in a Concorde.)

Elvis's coat of arms "Taking Care of Business", which is immortalized on his tombstone, has been transformed into the motto of his fans: "Taking Care of Elvis". Argus-eyed, they watch over Elvis's memory to ensure that it never fades.

Filmography

ELVIS PRESLEY FILMOGRAPHY

No.	Premiere	Min.	Songs	TITLE
1.	16. 11. 56	89	4	LOVE ME TENDER
2.	9. 7. 57	101	7	LOVING YOU
3.	21. 10. 57	96	7	JAILHOUSE ROCK
4.	4. 6. 58	115	13	KING CREOLE
5.	20. 10. 60	104	11	G.I. BLUES
6.	20. 12. 60	101	2	FLAMING STAR
7.	15. 6. 61	114	5	WILD IN THE COUNTRY
8.	14. 11. 61	101	15	BLUE HAWAII
9.	29. 3. 62	110	5	FOLLOW THAT DREAM
10.	25. 7. 62	95	6	KID GALAHAD
11.	2. 11. 62	106	14	GIRLS! GIRLS! GIRLS!
12.	3. 4. 63	105	10	IT HAPPENED AT THE WORLD'S FAIR
13.	21. 11. 63	98	11	FUN IN ACAPULCO
14.	6. 3. 64	96	9	KISSIN' COUSINS
15.	20. 4. 64	86	10	VIVA LAS VEGAS
16.	12. 11. 64	101	11	ROUSTABOUT
17.	21. 1. 65	96	11	GIRL HAPPY
18.	15. 6. 65	90	7	TICKLE ME
19.	15. 12. 65	95	9	HARUM SCARUM/HAREM HOLIDAY
20.	20. 7. 66	87	13	FRANKIE AND JOHNNY
21.	8. 6. 66	91	9	PARADISE, HAWAIIAN STYLE
22.	14. 12. 66	95	9	SPINOUT/CALIFORNIA HOLIDAY
23.	14. 6. 67	95	6	EASY COME, EASY GO
24.	24. 5. 67	90	8	DOUBLE TROUBLE
25.	4. 12. 67	99	7	CLAMBAKE
26.	14. 3. 68	98	4	STAY AWAY, JOE!
27.	13. 6. 68	90	7	SPEEDWAY
28.	9. 10. 68	89	4	LIVE A LITTLE, LOVE A LITTLE
29.	3. 9. 69	98	1	CHARRO
30.	10. 12. 69	99	2	THE TROUBLE WITH GIRLS
31.	21. 7. 70	93	4	CHANGE OF HABIT

2 documentary films about (and with) Elvis Presley

No.	Premiere	Min.	Songs	TITLE
32.	15. 12. 70	107	27	ELVIS: THAT'S THE WAY IT IS
33.	6. 6. 73	93	10	ELVIS ON TOUR